SELLING THINGS

THE MARDEN
INSPIRATIONAL BOOKS

Be Good to Yourself
Choosing a Career
Conquest of Worry
Every Man a King
The Exceptional Employee
Getting On
He Can Who Thinks He Can
How They Succeeded
How to Get What You Want
How to Succeed
Joys of Living
Keeping Fit
Little Visits With Great
    Americans
Love's Way
Making Friends With Our
    Nerves
Making Life a Masterpiece
Making Yourself

Masterful Personality
Miracle of Right Thought
Optimistic Life
Peace, Power, and Plenty
Progressive Business Man
Pushing to the Front
Rising in the World
Round Pegs in Square Holes
Secret of Achievement
Self-Investment
Selling Things
Success- A Book of Ideals
Success Fundamentals
Training for Efficiency
Victorious Attitude
Winning Out
Woman and the Home
You Can, But Will You?
The Young Man Entering
    Business

SPECIAL BOOKS AND BOOKLETS

An Iron Will   Opportunity   Self-Discovery
Economy   Cheerfulness   Hints for Young Writers
Thrift   Character- The Grandest Thing in the World
Success Nuggets   I Had a Friend   Why Grow Old?
Not the Salary, But the Opportunity
Ambition and Success   The Power of Personality
Good Manners- A Passport to Success   Thoughts About Character
Thoughts About Cheerfulness

The Life Story of Orison Swett Marden
By Margaret Connolly

A SELECT LIST OF SUN BOOKS TITLES

ORISON SWETT MARDEN BOOKS

AN IRON WILL
CHARACTER: The Grandest Thing in the World
THE EXCEPTIONAL EMPLOYEE
EVERY MAN A KING or MIGHT IN MIND-
   MASTERY
HE CAN WHO THINKS HE CAN
THE HOUR OF OPPORTUNITY
HOW THEY SUCCEEDED
HOW TO GET WHAT YOU WANT

THE MIRACLE OF RIGHT THOUGHT
THE OPTIMISTIC LIFE
PEACE, POWER, AND PLENTY
PUSHING TO THE FRONT 2 VOL SET
THE SECRET OF ACHIEVEMENT
SELLING THINGS
THE VICTORIOUS ATTITUDE
WHY GROW OLD?
YOU CAN, BUT WILL YOU?

JAMES ALLEN BOOKS

ABOVE LIFE'S TURMOIL
ALL THESE THINGS ADDED
AS A MAN THINKETH
EIGHT PILLARS OF PROSPERITY
FROM POVERTY TO POWER
THE LIFE TRIUMPHANT
LIGHT ON LIFE'S DIFFICULTIES
MAN: KING OF MIND, BODY AND
   CIRCUMSTANCE

THE MASTERY OF DESTINY
MEDITATIONS. A YEAR BOOK
MORNING AND EVENING THOUGHTS
OUT FROM THE HEART
THROUGH THE GATE OF GOOD
THE WAY OF PEACE
PERSONALITY: ITS CULTIVATION AND
   POWER AND HOW TO ATTAIN
   (by Lily L. Allen)

RALPH WALDO TRINE BOOKS

CHARACTER BUILDING THOUGHT POWER
EVERY LIVING CREATURE or Heart Training
   Through the Animal World
IN THE FIRE OF THE HEART
THE GREATEST THING EVER KNOWN

THE HIGHER POWERS OF MIND & SPIRIT
THE MAN WHO KNEW
ON THE OPEN ROAD - Being Some Thoughts
   and a Little Creed of Wholesome Living
THIS MYSTICAL LIFE OF OURS

ADDITIONAL IMPORTANT TITLES

BEING AND BECOMING: Principles and Practices of the Science of Spirit by F.L. Holmes.
CREATIVE MIND by Ernest S. Holmes.
HEALTH AND WEALTH FROM WITHIN by William E. Towne.
A MESSAGE TO GARCIA and Other Essays by Elbert Hubbard.
POSITIVE THOUGHTS ATTRACT SUCCESS by Mary A. Dodson and Ella E. Dodson.
THE SCIENCE OF GETTING RICH: or Financial Success Through Creative Thought.
SELF MASTERY THROUGH CONSCIOUS AUTOSUGGESTION by Emile Coué.
HOW TO PRACTICE SUGGESTION AND AUTOSUGGESTION by Emile Coué.
MY METHOD by Emile Coué.
THE SUCCESS PROCESS by Brown Landone.
THE GIFT OF THE SPIRIT by Prentice Mulford.
THE GIFT OF UNDERSTANDING by Prentice Mulford.
THOUGHT FORCES by Prentice Mulford.   THOUGHTS ARE THINGS by Prentice Mulford.
VISUALIZATION AND CONCENTRATION and How to Choose a Career by F.L. Holmes.

**For a list of all currently available Sun Books Inspirational Titles,
write to: Inspiration Catalog, PO Box 5588, Santa Fe NM 87502-5588**

SELLING THINGS

BY
ORISON SWETT MARDEN
AUTHOR OF "PUSHING TO THE FRONT," "PEACE, POWER AND PLENTY," "THE VICTORIOUS ATTITUDE," ETC.

WITH THE ASSISTANCE OF
JOSEPH F. MacGRAIL
INSTRUCTOR IN SALESMANSHIP AND EFFICIENCY FOR MANY LARGE SALES AND INDUSTRIAL ORGANIZATIONS

SUN BOOKS
Sun Publishing Company

First Sun Books Printing...1997

Copyright © 1997 By Sun Publishing Company

COPYRIGHT, 1916
BY THOMAS Y. CROWELL COMPANY

Sun Books
are Published by
Sun Publishing Company
P.O. Box 5588 Santa Fe,
NM 87502-5588 U.S.A.

ISBN: 0-89540-339-0

CONTENTS

CHAPTER		PAGE
I	THE MAN WHO CAN SELL THINGS	1
II	TRAINING THE SALESMAN	6
III	THE MOST IMPORTANT SUBJECTS OF STUDY	14
IV	MAKING A FAVORABLE IMPRESSION	19
V	THE SELLING TALK OR "PRESENTATION"	28
VI	THE APPROACH AND EXPRESSION	33
VII	THE ABILITY TO TALK WELL	37
VIII	HOW TO GET ATTENTION	42
IX	TACT AS A FRIEND-WINNER AND BUSINESS-GETTER	47
X	SIZING UP THE PROSPECT	62
XI	HOW SUGGESTION HELPS IN SELLING	71
XII	THE FORCE OF CHEERFUL EXPECTANCY	79
XIII	THE GENTLE ART OF PERSUASION	86
XIV	HELPING THE CUSTOMER TO BUY	94
XV	CLOSING THE DEAL	105
XVI	THE GREATEST SALESMAN—ENTHUSIASM	112
XVII	THE MAN AT THE OTHER END OF THE BARGAIN	119
XVIII	MEETING AND FORESTALLING OBJECTIONS	125
XIX	QUALITY AS A SALESMAN	133
XX	A SALESMAN'S CLOTHES	139
XXI	FINDING CUSTOMERS	148

CONTENTS

CHAPTER		PAGE
XXII	WHEN YOU ARE DISCOURAGED . . .	155
XXIII	THE STIMULUS OF REBUFFS	163
XXIV	MEETING COMPETITION: "KNOW YOUR GOODS"	177
XXV	THE SALESMAN AND THE SALES MANAGER	184
XXVI	ARE YOU A GOOD MIXER?	189
XXVII	CHARACTER IS CAPITAL	207
XXVIII	THE PRICE OF MASTERSHIP	213
XXIX	KEEPING FIT AND SALESMANSHIP . .	226
	APPENDIX—SALES POINTERS	250

SELLING THINGS

SELLING THINGS

CHAPTER I

THE MAN WHO CAN SELL THINGS

Cultivate all the arts and all the helps to mastership.

The world always listens to a man with a will in him.

Soon after Henry Ward Beecher went to Plymouth Church he received a letter from a Western parish, asking him to send them a new pastor. After describing the sort of man they wanted, the letter closed with the following injunction: "BE SURE TO SEND US A MAN WHO CAN SWIM. Our last pastor was drowned while fording the river, on a visit to his parishioners."

Now, this is the sort of a man that is wanted everywhere, in every line of human activity, *the man who can swim,* the salesman who can swim, who can sell things, who can go out and get business, the man who can take a message

SELLING THINGS

to Garcia, who can bring back the order, the man who can "deliver the goods."

The whole business world to-day is hunting for the man who can sell things; there is a sign up at every manufacturing establishment, every producing establishment for the man who can market products. There is nobody in greater demand than the efficient salesman, and he is rarely if ever out of a job.

Only a short while ago two companies actually went to law about a salesman who transferred his connection from one to the other, his original employers holding that he had no right to do so, as he was under contract (at a $50,000 salary) to them.

In spite of the fact that thousands of employees are looking for positions, on every hand we see employers looking for somebody who can "deliver the goods"; a salesman who will not say that if conditions were right, if everything were favorable, if it were not for the panic, or some other stumbling block, he could sell the goods. Everywhere employers are looking for some one who can do things, no matter what the conditions may be.

There is no place in salesmanship for the

THE MAN WHO CAN SELL THINGS 3

man who waits for orders to come to him. He is simply an order taker, not a salesman. Live men, men with vigorous initiative and lots of pluck and grit, men who can go out and get business are wanted.

It should not be necessary to prove that training is needed for success in salesmanship or in any business. Yet, because men have been compelled for centuries "to learn by their mistakes," to pick up here and there, by hard knocks, a little knowledge about their work, there has been a prejudice against trying to teach business by sane, scientific methods. Besides, in former times, the working man and the mere merchant were supposed to belong to a low class of society, apart from the noble and the learned, and little attention was given to their needs. A man, too, was believed to be born with a natural aptitude for salesmanship or business building, and this was supposed to be all-sufficient.

To-day there are many men and women attracted by the big profits in salesmanship, who would like to become salesmen and saleswomen, but they feel they have not this natural aptitude to insure permanent success.

SELLING THINGS

It is true that, just as certain men and women are born with natural gifts for music and for art, so certain men and women have, in a high degree, the natural qualities which enable them to succeed in selling either their brain power or merchandise. But while it is true that some people have more natural capacity than others, it is not true to-day, and it was never true in the fine arts, in athletics, or in commercial pursuits, that the untrained man is the equal of the trained man.

Man is always improving Nature, or, if you prefer, he is always helping Nature. Central Park, New York, is more beautiful because the landscape gardener has been helping Nature; the farmer is the reaper of bigger and better crops because he is following the advice of the chemist, who tells him how to fertilize the soil; the Delaware River and Hell Gate have become more easily navigable, because the engineer has removed obstacles which Nature had placed in those waters; Colorado's arid lands are irrigated, thanks to the skill of the civil engineer; the horticulturist aids Nature by grafting and pruning; the scientist comes to the help of human nature with antiseptic methods in surgery; and the inventor

THE MAN WHO CAN SELL THINGS 5

shows Nature how electricity can be put to numberless practical uses.

Let us not fool ourselves; we need to study, we need to be trained for every business in life. And in these days the training by which natural defects are overcome and natural aptitude is developed into effective ability can be obtained by every youth. No matter how great your natural ability in any direction, in order to get the best results, it must be reënforced by this special training.

The untrained man may get results here and there because he has natural ability and unconsciously uses the right methods. The trained man is getting results regularly because he is consistently using the right methods.

Business men no longer attribute a lost sale, where it should have been made, to "hard luck," but to ignorance of the science of salesmanship.

The "born" salesman is not as much in vogue as formerly. Business is becoming a science, and almost any honest, dead-in-earnest, determined youth can become an expert in it, if he is willing to pay the price.

It is scientific salesmanship to-day, and not luck, that gets the order.

CHAPTER II

TRAINING THE SALESMAN

The consciousness of being superbly equipped for your work brings untold satisfaction.

Efficiency is the watchword of to-day. The half-prepared man, the man who is ignorant, the man who doesn't know his lines, is placed at a tremendous disadvantage.

A STUDENT seeking admission to Oberlin College asked its famous president if there was not some way of taking a sort of homeopathic college course, some short-cut by which he could get all the essentials in a few months.

This was the president's reply: *"When the Creator wanted a squash, he created it in six months, but when he wanted an oak, he took a hundred years."*

One of the highest-paid women workers in the world, the foreign buyer for a big department store, owes her position more to thorough training for her work than to any other thing. Between salary and commissions, her income amounts to thirty thousand dollars a year.

Training the Salesman

Speaking of her place in the firm, one of its highest members said to a writer: "We regard Miss Blank as more of a friend than an employee; and she came to us just twenty years ago with her hair in pig-tails, tied with a shoe string; and she was so ill fed and ill clothed we had to pass her over to our house nurse to get her currycombed and scrubbed before we could put her on as a cash girl. Without training, she would probably have dropped back in the gutter as an unfit and a failure. With training, she has become one of the ablest business women in the country."

There are a thousand pigmy salesmen to one Napoleon salesman; but if you have natural ability for the marketing of any of the great products of the world, all you need to make you a Napoleon salesman is sound training and willingness to work faithfully. With such a foundation for success you will not long be out of a job, or remain in obscurity, for wherever you go, no matter how hard the times, you will see an advertisement for just such a man.

The term "salesmanship" is a very broad one; it covers many fields. The drummer for

SELLING THINGS

a boot and shoe house, the insurance agent and manager, the banker and broker, whose business is to dispose of millions of dollars' worth of stocks and bonds—all these are "salesmen," trafficking in one kind of goods or another—all form a part of the world's great system of organized barter.

There are three essentials which must be considered in deciding on salesmanship or any other vocation, namely: taste, talent, and training. The first is, by far, the most important of these essentials, for whatever we have a taste for, we will be interested in; what we really become interested in, we are bound to love, sooner or later, and success comes from loving our work.

To find out whether or not you are cut out for a salesman, you must first analyze the question of your taste and your talent. In this matter, however, it should be borne in mind that human nature, especially in youth, is plastic, and that we can be molded by others, or we can mold ourselves. Even though one has not a strong taste, naturally, or a decided talent for salesmanship, he can acquire both, for even talent, like taste, may be

TRAINING THE SALESMAN

either natural or acquired. By proper training in salesmanship, which means the right kind of reading, observing and listening, and right practicing, we can develop our taste and ability so as to become good salesmen or good saleswomen.

The basic requirements for successful salesmanship are good health, a cheerful disposition, courtesy, tact, resourcefulness, facility of expression, honesty, a firm and unshakable confidence in one's self, a thorough knowledge of, and confidence in, the goods which one is selling, and ability to close. True cordiality of manner must be reënforced by intelligence and by a ready command of information in regard to the matters in hand. It will be seen that all these things make the *man* as well as the salesman—when coupled with sincerity and highmindedness, they can't but bring success in any career.

The foundation for salesmanship can hardly be laid too early. The youth who uses his spare time when at school, in vacation season, and out of business hours, in acquiring the art of salesmanship will gain power to climb up in the world that cannot be obtained so readily by any other means.

SELLING THINGS

Fortunate is the young man who has received the right kind of business training. No matter what his occupation or profession, such training will make him a more efficient worker. Many youths have had fathers whose experience and advice have been valuable to them. Others have been favored by getting into firms of high caliber. As a result they have been in a splendid environment during their most formative years, and in so far have had an inestimable advantage in success training.

Many people have the impression that almost anybody can be a salesman, and that salesmanship doesn't require much, if any, special training. The young man who starts out to sell things on this supposition will soon find out his mistake. If salesmanship is to be your vocation you cannot afford to take any such superficial view of its requirements. You cannot afford to botch your life. You cannot afford a little, picayune career as a salesman, with a little salary and no outlook. If salesmanship is worth giving your life to, it is worth very serious and very profound and scientific preparation and training.

I know a physician, a splendid fellow, who

TRAINING THE SALESMAN

studied medicine in a small, country medical school, where there was very little material, and practically no opportunity for hospital work. In fact, during his years of preparation his experience outside of medical books was very meager. Since getting his M. D. diploma this man has been a very hard worker and has managed to get a fair living, but he is much handicapped in his chance to make a name in his profession. He has a fine mind, however, and if he had gone to the Harvard Medical School in Boston, or to one of the other great medical schools where there is an abundance of material for observation and facilities for practice in the hospitals and clinics, he would have learned more in six months, outside of what he gathered from books and lectures, than he learned in all of his course in the country medical schools. His poor training has condemned him to a mediocre success, when his natural ability, with a thorough preparation, would have made him a noted physician.

You cannot afford to carry on your life work as an amateur, with improper preparation. You want to be known as an expert, as a man of standing, a man who would be looked

SELLING THINGS

up to as an authority, a specialist in his line. To enter on your life work indifferently prepared, half trained, would be like a man going into business without even a common school education, knowing nothing about figures. No matter how naturally able such a man might be, people would take advantage of his ignorance. He would be at the mercy of his bookkeeper and other employees, and of unscrupulous business men. And if he should try to make up for his lack of early training or education, he must do it at a great cost in time and energy.

Successful salesmanship of the highest order requires not only a fine special training, but also a good education and a keen insight into human nature; it also requires resourcefulness, inventiveness and originality. In fact, a salesman who would become a giant in his line, must combine with the art of salesmanship a number of the highest intellectual qualities.

Yet in salesmanship, as in every other vocation, there is not one qualification needed that can not be cultivated by any youth of average ability and intelligence. Success in it, as in every other business and profession, is merely

TRAINING THE SALESMAN 13

the triumph of the common virtues and ordinary ability.

In salesmanship, as in war, there is offensive and defensive. The trained salesman knows how to attack, and he knows how to defend himself when he is attacked. Everything contained within the covers of this book has for its object the most effective offensive and defensive methods in selling.

CHAPTER III

THE MOST IMPORTANT SUBJECTS OF STUDY

"Salesmanship is knowing yourself, your company, your prospect and your product, and applying your knowledge."

The qualities which make a great business man also enter into the making of a great salesman.

Salesmanship is fast becoming a profession, and only the salesman who is superbly equipped can hope to win out in any large way.

DIFFERENT authorities agree pretty much on the subjects which must be studied or understood in the making of good salesmen, although they classify in somewhat different ways the headings under which salesmanship should be studied.

Mr. Arthur F. Sheldon, for instance, in his able Course, has divided the knowledge pertaining to scientific salesmanship under four heads: 1, The Salesman; 2, The Goods; 3, The Customer; 4, The Sale. The "Drygoods Economist" has some excellent courses on salesmanship, in which they use almost this

Most Important Subjects of Study 15

identical classification, treating the subject under the four general divisions: 1, The Salesman; 2, The Goods; 3, The Customer; 4, Service. Mr. Charles L. Huff has added to the valuable data on salesmanship a book in which he gives the following five factors as the headings under which the subject of salesmanship should be covered, namely: 1, Price; 2, Quality; 3, Service; 4, Friendship; 5, Presentation.

Every salesman is really teaching the customer something about the goods. He is, so to speak, a teacher of values, or if you prefer, "a business missionary." In order to teach well he should have these most valuable assets: first, right methods of meeting customer; second, thorough knowledge of self, of goods, of customer and conditions; third, ability to meet competition, both real and imaginary; fourth, helpful habits; fifth, good powers of originating and planning; sixth, a selling talk, or something worth while saying; seventh, properly developed feelings, which will add force to what he says.

In a brief and helpful course on salesmanship "System," a business magazine, gives

SELLING THINGS

great emphasis to the value of dwelling on five buying motives—1, Money; 2, Utility; 3, Caution; 4, Pride; 5, Self-Indulgence, or Yielding to Weakness.

If a salesman will keep before his mind these five points, and if he appeals to the human traits they indicate he will become a master in closing deals.

A great many methods are used to-day for rating employees, just as Dun and Bradstreet rate firms. According to Roger W. Babson, there is a Mr. Horner, of Minneapolis, who rates his salesmen and trains them along these lines:

HABITS OF WORK

1. Idealism

2. Intelligence
   - a. Understanding of business
   - b. Selecting policy to suit age and condition of applicant
   - c. Self-culture.

3. Hopefulness
4. Optimism

5. Uniform courtesy
   - a. To clients
   - b. To office force
   - c. To fellow agents

6. Number of daily interviews
7. Concentration or effectiveness of work, as to waste of time or energy.

Most Important Subjects of Study 17

8. Loyalty { a. To company
             b. To organization
             c. To fellow agents
9. Attention to old policy holders
10. Enthusiasm.

A final. and very vital point to consider is this: Why do salesmen meet opposition?

Mr. Huff, in his very practical and interesting book on salesmanship, has classified under six general heads the causes of opposition. These are: First, Prior Dissatisfaction; Second, General Prejudice; Third, Buyer's Mood; Fourth, Conservatism; Fifth, Bad Business; Sixth, Personal Dislike for Salesman.

It is up to the salesman to analyze the customer and decide just which of these six points of opposition is causing him to lose business.

Just in the degree that he can locate the exact trouble, and then overcome it in the proper way, will he be able to get the business which may seem at first absolutely beyond him.

Any or all of these six causes of opposition will not overwhelm the master salesman, but the mediocre or indifferent salesman is bound to collapse when confronted with any one of

18   SELLING THINGS

them.   And if he does not train himself to meet and overcome opposition he is doomed to failure, or at least to a very poor grade of success—not worthy the name.

Remember, Mr. Salesman, it is always up to you.   Develop your brain power, and then use that power for all it is worth.

CHAPTER IV

MAKING A FAVORABLE IMPRESSION

Go boldly; go serenely, go augustly;
Who can withstand thee then!

BROWNING.

The personality of a salesman is his greatest asset.

A WASHINGTON government official called on me some time ago, and before he had reached my desk I knew he was a man of importance, on an important mission. He had that assured bearing which indicated that he was backed by authority—in this instance the authority of the United States—and the dignity of his bearing and manner commanded my instant respect and attention.

The impression you make as you enter a prospect's office will greatly influence the manner of your reception. It is imperative to make a favorable first impression, otherwise you will have to spend much valuable time and energy and suffer a great deal of embarrassment in trying to right yourself in your pros-

20 SELLING THINGS

pect's estimation, because he will not do business with you until you have made a favorable impression on him.

Some salesmen approach their prospect with such an apologetic, cringing, "excuse me for taking up your valuable time" air, that they give him the idea they are not on a very important mission, and that they are not sure of themselves, that they have not much confidence in the firm they represent or the merchandise they are trying to sell.

Approach the one with whom you expect to do business like a man, without any doubts, without any earmarks of a cringing, crawling or craven disposition. Enter his office as the Washington official entered mine, like a high-class man meeting a high-class man. You will compel attention and respect instantly, as he did.

Your introduction is an entering wedge, your first chance to score a point. If you present a pleasing picture as you enter you will score a strong point. Here is where you must choose the golden mean between cringing and over-boldness. If you approach a man with your hat on, and a cigar or cigarette

Making a Favorable Impression 21

in your mouth, or still smoking in your fingers; if your breath smells of liquor; if you show that you are not up to physical standard; if there is any evidence of dissipation in your appearance; if you swagger or show any lack of respect, all these things will count against you. If you present an unpleasing picture, if there is anything about you which your prospect does not like; if you bluster, or if you lack dignity; if you do not look him straight in the eye; if there is any evidence of doubt or fear or lack of confidence in yourself, you will at once arouse a prejudice in his mind that will cause him to doubt the story you tell and to look with suspicion at the goods you are trying to sell.

A salesman once entered a business man's office holding a toothpick in his mouth. You may think it was a little thing, but it so prejudiced the would-be customer against him at the start that it made it much more difficult for him even to get a chance to show his samples. The business man in question was very particular in regard to little points of manners, and was himself a model of deportment.

I know of another salesman who makes a

SELLING THINGS

most unfortunate first impression because he has no presence whatever, not a particle of dignity; he is timid and morbidly self-conscious, and it takes him some minutes after he has met a stranger to regain his self-possession. To those who know him he is a kindly and genuinely lovable man, but he does not appear to advantage at a first introduction. He is a college graduate, and was so popular and stood so high in his class that he was proposed to represent it at commencement. He was defeated, however, on the plea that he would make such a bad impression on the public that he would not properly represent the class.

Self-possession is an indispensable quality in a salesman. It is natural to the man who has confidence in himself, and without self-confidence it is hard to make a dignified appearance or to make others believe in you.

What you think of yourself will have a great deal to do with what a prospect will think of you, because you will radiate your estimate of yourself. If you have a little seven-by-nine model of a man in your mind you will etch that picture on the mind of your pros-

MAKING A FAVORABLE IMPRESSION 23

pect. In approaching a prospect, walk, talk and act not only like a man who believes in himself, but one who also believes in and thoroughly knows his business. When a physician is called into a home in an emergency, no matter how able a man may be at the head of the house, no matter how well educated the mother and children may be, everybody stands aside when he enters. They feel that the doctor is the master of the situation, that he alone knows what to do, and they all defer to him. Everybody follows his directions implicitly.

You should approach a possible customer with something of this professional air, an air of supreme assurance, of confidence in your ability, in your honesty and integrity, confidence in your knowledge of your business. Your professional dignity alone will help to make a good impression, and will win courtesy. It will insure you at least a respectful hearing, and there is your chance to play your part in a masterful manner.

A publisher who has a large number of book agents in the field, advises his men to act, when the servant answers the door bell, as though they were expected and welcome. He tells

SELLING THINGS

them, if it is raining to take off their rubbers, if it is muddy or dusty to wipe off their shoes and act as though they expected to go in.

The idea is to make a favorable impression upon the servant first of all, for if they were to behave as though they were not sure they would be admitted, apologizing for making so much trouble and assuming the attitude of asking a favor, they would communicate their doubt to the servant, and would not be likely to gain admittance, not to speak of an audience with the mistress. In short, the carrying of a positive, victorious mental attitude, the radiating of a vigorous expectation of getting a hearing will get you one.

The agent who rings a door bell with a palpitating heart, with a great big doubt in his mind as to whether he ought to do it, and who, when the door is opened, acts as though he were stealing somebody's valuable time, and had no right to be there at all, will create a prejudice against him before he opens his mouth. And before he gets a chance to plead his cause he will probably find the door closed in his face.

You should seek admission to a house as though you were the bearer of glad tidings, as

Making a Favorable Impression   25

though you had good news for the family, as though you were conferring a real favor on them by calling their attention to what you have to sell.

Whatever you are selling, whether books or pianos, hardware or drygoods, your manner will largely determine the amount of your sales. There are salesmen who approach prospective customers just as though they not only did not expect an order, but rather expected, if not to get kicked out, at least a polite invitation to get out.

I was in the office of a business man recently, when a man of this stamp came in and crept up to him with a sort of a sheepish expression on his face, as much as to say, "I know I haven't any right here, but I have come in to ask for a favor, which I feel sure you won't grant."

"I don't suppose you have an order for me to-day, have you?" he said. Of course, the man, without a moment's hesitation, said, "No." And the salesman crept out as though he had almost committed a sin by entering at all.

Now, there is something in every manly man

which despises this self-depreciating spirit, this false self-effacement, this creeping, cringing, apologizing attitude, which robs one of all dignity and power. If you approach people as though you expected a kick, you are pretty sure to get it. It may come in the form of a gruff refusal, of a snub, or of a polite invitation to get out, but you are likely to get what you invite—a rebuff of some kind.

If you approach a man at all, do it in a brave, vigorous, manly way. Do not ruin your cause by giving him a contemptible picture of you at the very outset. At least let him see that you are self-respecting, manly, that there is nothing of the coward in you. Even if he declines to give you an order, compel him to respect you, to admire you for your dignified, virile bearing. No one cares to do business with a person he cannot help despising, while a man who creates a favorable impression will at least get a hearing.

We recently asked a representative of a big concern how he managed to do so much business with people whom very few salesmen can approach.

"Well," he said, "I will tell you. One reason is that I never go to a man as though

Making a Favorable Impression 27

I had no right to. I do not creep into his office and look as though I expected a kick or a rebuff. I walk right straight up to him in the most manly and commanding way possible, for I am bound to make a good impression on him, so that he will remember me pleasantly, even if I do not get an order. The result is that men who are very difficult to approach often give me business they refuse to others because I am not afraid to approach them and to say what I want to say pleasantly, without mincing or cringing or apologizing."

This man says he has little difficulty in getting into the private offices of the most exclusive business men, presidents of banks, great financiers, high officials of railroads and other representatives of "big business," and that they are his best customers.

To sum up, your attitude, the spirit you radiate, your personality, will have everything to do with your salesmanship. The impression you make will be a tremendous factor in your sales. For this reason you should never approach a prospect until you feel that you are master of the situation. Then you will carry the conviction and give the impression of mastership, and that is half the battle.

CHAPTER V

THE SELLING TALK OR "PRESENTATION"

Talk to the point; talk with reason; talk with force; talk with conviction.

Let your selling talk be direct, natural, and as brief as possible.

MUCH has been written on the question of a selling talk, and there is no little misunderstanding on this all-important subject. Every one who has "a story to tell" has what may be called "a selling talk"; that is to say, a best way of setting forth what he has in his mind. Some prefer to call it the "presentation." A "presentation" may consist of a few sentences, or it may consist of a half hour's talk. Salesmen in many lines cannot prepare a fixed story or address, such as would be given by a statesman addressing a legislative body, or by a clergyman in a sermon, or by an actor giving a monologue, and yet, large numbers of salesmen, through failing to have a simple, clear, carefully worded talk, fail to get a

Selling Talk or "Presentation" 29

customer interested in their merchandise. The question of a selling talk should be left to the judgment of the sales manager. He will be well qualified, ordinarily, to tell just what this should consist of, and, also, when to make exceptions to the use of a selling talk. Inspiration will not come just when the salesman wants it. Many points get lost in the convolutions of the brain. Too much or too little talk may be indulged in, unless a salesman knows just what he is going to say and how to say it. Do not be misled, however; there are many men who speak poor English, and who do not have what would properly be called a "selling talk," yet they succeed as salesmen. These men do, however, know the merits of their goods, and they have a peculiar way of putting it up to the customer to judge for himself.

I once saw nearly a thousand dollars' worth of underwear sold, with scarcely a word spoken. The salesman spread out his goods, and the buyer examined them hastily, but carefully, and made the selection, simply asking by what number the goods were known, and the price. I saw not long ago, about five thousand dollars' worth of furs (muffs and neck-pieces) bought, with very few words spoken. In both these cases it must be remembered that buyers and sellers were well known to each other; there was mutual confidence; the houses were reliable, and unsatisfactory goods would mean loss of future business, as well as a return of the goods.

There are certain main selling points which can be selected and should be selected for every line of goods. Some of these selling points will be more effective with one class of customers than with another. Here is where the salesman's judgment comes into play. Let us take the single example of the white goods business. In this line, there are five main selling points which I once heard given by Charles A. Sherman, of Sherman & Sons, leading merchants, of New York. These five points are:

1. Artistic merit of goods, beauty of design, etc.;
2. Intrinsic value;
3. Comparison with rival goods;
4. Degree of conformity to prevailing modes or fashions.
5. Adaptability to buyers' needs, price, etc.

Selling Talk or "Presentation" 31

Around these may be woven a brief or a lengthy talk, according to the needs and the disposition of the customer with whom the salesman is talking. Let your selling talk be direct, natural, and as brief as possible.

The presentation of your proposition involves, principally, a clear, simple and suitable description of your goods. The cleverest salesmen arrange the points in a logical order, working up from the least importance to the strongest.

Always put the question of price off just as long as possible, unless the price is so low that this point alone adds much to the other selling points, as for instance, setting forth the prices in a 5 & 10 cent store, or giving the prices of special bargains.

Be willing to answer all questions and objections made by your customer, but forestall, as far as you can, the objections he is likely to make. You can do this by exerting the power of a strong personality, especially by showing much enthusiasm, which tends to burn up the objections a customer is inclined to make. No matter how positive or how graphic you are in your descriptions, always be natural, otherwise your mannerisms will detract from the effectiveness of your talk.

The best authorities consider it a decided handicap if the customer "turned you down" at the start by a negative answer, or a negative attitude. When you foresee that the customer is about to say, "No," or to turn away, strive to keep his mind in the balance until you can attract his attention to some new features of your goods, or to some old features, in a new way.

The length of time given to a presentation, will vary with the goods and with the customer. Experience with each particular line, and the advice of your sales manager always should be followed.

On the floor of the Stock Exchange there is no such thing as a presentation, or the getting of favorable attention, in the strict interpretation we give to these words. Men are there alert to give favorable attention to certain securities. They know in advance the strong points of these securities, and when the right price is quoted the decision to buy will come quickly. This holds true in many instances where staple goods are offered at current prices.

CHAPTER VI

THE APPROACH AND EXPRESSION

No matter how well posted a man may be in the science and technique of salesmanship, his actual sales will depend very largely upon his personality.

"THE man or woman wishing to present to me a business proposition," said a high class, successful merchant, "must have a good address and an agreeable manner and appearance, or he will not get a hearing. The reason is, it would be impossible for me to see half the people who approach me with schemes; therefore, I reject without a hearing all those that are not presented by people who have an agreeable manner and good address. I take it for granted that a first-class proposition will be presented by a first-class man, and *vice versa.*"

Whether the customer comes to you, or you go to the customer, there are certain very simple things to keep in mind. The first is the important part personality plays in selling.

34 SELLING THINGS

The appearance and the manner of a salesman, together with the tactful enthusiasm which he manifests, and the concentration which he puts into his work, all tend to inspire confidence. The salesman must consider his customer's business, and sometimes his social position. The temperament, also, of the customer, as well as the best time and place to see him, must be taken into consideration. One of the things so often neglected by salesmen is to get points of contact from the surroundings, such as pictures on the wall, books and papers on the desk, as well as from the prospect's attire. Keep in mind these four aids to a right approach:

First: Entertain a feeling of equality with your customer.

Second: Remember that you have a favor to bestow. Assume the rôle of a benefactor.

Third: Show friendliness. There should be the heart-touch in every real approach.

Fourth: Be observing. Look for suggestions in your surroundings, for a point of contact.

We express ourselves not only through the words we utter, but by the tone of the voice,

The Approach and Expression 35

the expression of the face, our gestures, and our bearing. All five of these elements should be carefully considered, because the salesman who would have the greatest success not only must be understood, but he must be felt. It is important to be clear and forceful in our language, and for this purpose a thorough knowledge of English grammar and rhetoric will aid the salesman.

The accompanying chart should prove helpful.

EXPRESSION

"When all is said and done, it is the *choice and use of words* that determines whether or not we succeed in expressing our thoughts and feelings clearly and adequately."—"Manual of Composition and Rhetoric," by Gardiner, Kittredge and Arnold.

The five elements affecting expression of ideas are:

1. Voice
   - Rich,
   - Refined,
   - Deep,
   - Modulated,
   - Full, distinct articulation.

2. Bearing
   - Before sale,
   - During "
   - After "

3. Gestures
   - In talking,
   - " displaying samples,
   - " presenting reading matter or contracts.

4. Facial expression.

36 SELLING THINGS

5. Language
- *Diction* simple suitable
  - a. Purity — Violated by
    1. Slang;
    2. Obsolete words;
    3. Provincialisms;
    4. Foreign words;
    5. Newly coined words.
  - b. Precision — Results from
    1. Thorough knowledge of subject;
    2. Extensive vocabulary;
    3. Power to discriminate;
    4. Use of specific for general, or general for specific term, as idea requires.
- *Style* simple suitable
  - a. Unity — One idea at a time; Stick to subject.
  - b. Clearness — Have clear ideas and use appropriate words. Use good grammar. Beware of technical words.
  - c. Energy or Force — Results from brevity, clearness, directness and judicious use of figurative language.
  - d. Elegance or Harmony — Smooth, euphonious speech; Alliteration. Read best authors.

CHAPTER VII

THE ABILITY TO TALK WELL

"Words have worth, only when properly expressed."

It is the conquest, the conquest of the heart, by words that speak kindliness and assure confidence, which distinguishes the prosperous salesman, justly proud and progressive.

HENRY FRANK.

MANY a man with a good brain fails as a salesman, or remains a mediocre one, because he has never learned to express himself with ease and fluency. A lame, hesitating, poverty-stricken speech is fatal.

The ability to talk well is to a man what cutting and polishing are to the rough diamond. The grinding does not add anything to the diamond. It merely reveals its wealth.

It is an excellent thing to cultivate readiness in conversation, for this will incidentally develop other powers.

Every salesman should have a good broad working vocabulary. To hesitate and feel one's way for words in trying to make a sale

38 SELLING THINGS

is fatal. The salesman must express himself easily, clearly, and forcefully, otherwise he will be placed at a certain disadvantage. He must be not only a fluent talker, but also a convincing one.

The ability to talk well is a great aid to success in any line of endeavor, but if our heads are empty, mere facility in words will not help us much. Not "words, words, words," but "points, points, points" win. This is especially true in salesmanship.

A good salesman should be well read on general topics as well as in his special line. There is no other way in which a person will reveal a shallow or a full mind, a narrow or a broad one, a well-read or a poverty-stricken mentality so quickly as in his speech.

To be a good conversationalist, able to interest people, to rivet their attention, to draw them to you naturally, is to be the possessor of a very great and valuable accomplishment. It not only helps you to make a good impression upon strangers, it also helps you to make and keep friends. It opens doors and softens hearts. It makes you interesting in all sorts of company. It helps you marvelously to get

The Ability to Talk Well 39

on in the world. It sends you customers, it attracts business.

It is a deplorable fact that indifference of speech is one of the characteristics of the American people. We are not only poor conversationalists, but we are poor listeners as well. We are too impatient to listen. Instead of being attentive and eager to drink in the story or the information, we have not enough respect for the talker to keep quiet. We look about impatiently, perhaps snap our watch, play a tattoo with our fingers on a chair or a table, twitch about as if we were bored and were anxious to get away, and frequently interrupt the speaker before he reaches his conclusion. In fact, we are such an impatient people that we have no time for anything except to push ahead, to elbow our way through the crowd, to get the position or the money we desire.

Poor conversationalists excuse themselves for not trying to improve by saying that "good talkers are born, not made." We might as well say that good lawyers, good physicians, good merchants or good salesmen are born, not made. None of these would ever get very far

40 SELLING THINGS

without hard work. This is the price of all achievement that is of value.

To be a good talker one must be a good observer, a good listener, a good reader, a good thinker, and a clear speaker. It will not do to mumble or to slur over your words. You should speak distinctly, plainly, and not too rapidly. Don't talk like a drone or a parrot. Put force, thought and feeling into your words; fill them full of meaning, so that people will want to hear what you say.

You know what an impression a great orator makes upon an audience when he measures his words and sends them out with deliberation, with feeling and force. They are infinitely more impressive than the excited, impassioned shouting, which comes from an over-wrought mind.

Readiness in conversation is largely a matter of practice. But the voice, especially the American voice, needs to be trained.

There is nothing more disagreeable than a harsh, discordant voice, unless it be the high-pitched, nasal intonation so characteristic of our people, or the whine which is frequently heard from those who are narrow-minded and

THE ABILITY TO TALK WELL 41

discontented. A low, clear, well-modulated voice indicates refinement and should be carefully cultivated by the salesman who wishes to express himself forcefully.

It is very difficult to convince a prospect that he should buy your merchandise when you are pleading your cause either in high-pitched, sharp, shrill tones, or in mumbling or nasal ones which have no magnetism, no attractiveness in them.

A clear, deep, melodious voice tends to unlock minds and to win confidence, while a harsh, shrill, discordant voice antagonizes us.

The ability to talk well, to interest and hold others, increases our self-respect, our confidence, and gains us a ready entrance to places from which we would otherwise be excluded. If you expect to be a first-class salesman, a man of power in any line of endeavor you should cultivate your voice and practice the art of conversation.

CHAPTER VIII

HOW TO GET ATTENTION

You must interest your customer before you can hope to influence him.

"Shape your argument in harmony with conditions; don't try to force a square block into a round hole."

THERE are three principal ways in which to get the favorable attention of a prospect; the first is "affording pleasure;" the second, "exciting admiration," and the third, "arousing curiosity." As often as possible we should combine all three.

If our words and our expression radiate genuine, cheerful good-will, then the customer is pleased to meet us. We can cause him to be still more pleased, if we praise, in a very tactful way, some of the good qualities which we quickly observe in him.

Our appearance, from head to foot, is what causes admiration. We should always be well groomed; hair properly cut and carefully arranged; teeth well cared for; eyes bright;

HOW TO GET ATTENTION 43

linen immaculate; clothes well pressed; cuffs and collar free from frayed edges. Loud colors and loud jewelry always detract from the power of the salesman. Heels that are not run down, and shoes that are well polished, are final factors to consider.

We arouse a customer's curiosity by asking him suitable questions. It is a good idea to prepare him for the kind of an answer you expect, by some positive suggestion, before you ask the question. For instance, a man who wishes to sell a beautiful piece of jewelry can say: "I consider this a very beautiful stone, which has been set most artistically." Then he can say to the customer; "What do you think of that jewel?" Invariably, the customer will tend to agree with him, and this helps to get their minds together.

The late Elbert Hubbard used to say that he always began an advertisement with the statement of an incontrovertible fact. The public read it and agreed. It could give rise to no antagonistic or opposing train of thought. It established a coördinate bond between the writer of the ad. and the reader. Then Hubbard followed with statements concerning the article advertised. With these the reader might not agree, but at least he started reading the ad. in a friendly spirit.

Remember this: it is never best to begin to talk much about your goods until you have secured real attention, not simply a civil attention, for courtesy's sake, but the genuine thing. Real attention is "a thought spiller and a thought filler." The customer "spills" his thoughts, and "fills" in the salesman's thoughts.

Some salesmen have found it a big advantage to get the customer to do some little thing for them, such as holding a sample, loaning a pencil, getting a piece of paper on which to figure, etc. Requests for favors of this kind, however, must be made in a tactful way. The idea back of this ingenious method is to start the will of the customer acting according to the salesmen's will.

If the moment seems favorable you should take the order at once and dispense with all salesman's art; but after taking the order, proceed to strengthen the customer in his decision by calling attention to certain strong points of merit in your goods, and certain

How to Get Attention 45

strong reasons which you believe will make the customer glad he has made his purchase. Be careful, however, to avoid over-talking. This is a blunder that has cost many a man dear.

The art of a salesman shows itself in his ability to focus his energies quickly and to size up his prospect in many respects at a glance. He must see what kind of a temperament he has to deal with. He must know what to do and what to say to each particular man. Before entering a strange office he has no idea what sort of a man will confront him, whether one who is fat or lean, of a nervous or a phlegmatic temperament, whether vigorous or in delicate health, whether a thin-skinned, sensitive man or one of a coarse type with a rhinoceros hide.

In calling on regular customers, the salesman must be alert for passing whims that modify their disposition. He must take in a man's mood at a glance. If he is in a bad mood, he cannot approach him as if he were in a happy mood, as though he had just had some good news. He must be able to tell by his appearance whether he is pleased because business is booming, or whether he is dis-

46 SELLING THINGS

gruntled, his mind clouded either by business or domestic troubles. In fact, a salesman must be able to recognize quickly and deal adequately with all sorts of men and moods, and business conditions, or he will fail at the start to get the sort of attention on which his sales depend.

CHAPTER IX

TACT AS A FRIEND-WINNER AND BUSINESS-GETTER

Tact eases the jolts, oils the bearings, opens doors barred to others, sits in the drawing-room when others wait in the reception hall, gets into the private office when others are turned down.

Whether you get an order or not, leave a good taste in your prospect's mouth so that he will always have a pleasant recollection of you.

SOME time ago a man and his wife went into a large store in an eastern city to buy a chandelier. The man, in a rather querulous tone, asked to be shown a Renaissance chandelier. "Now, be sure," he said to the salesman, "to show me a real Renaissance, small and not too expensive." The salesman perceived he had a difficult customer to deal with, but one who appeared to have a fixed idea in mind. Being extremely tactful, he knew his first task was to humor his customer, and then try to find out exactly what type of fixture had been pictured in his mind. By cordiality and an ex-

47

48 SELLING THINGS

change of remarks on general subjects, the salesman eased the man's mind, and by skillful questions found out exactly what sort of chandelier he wanted. Then he expressed himself pleased at having a customer with clear ideas about the sort of article he wished, as it made it so much easier for the salesman to suit him.

Only tact could ever have won over that man and satisfied his whim.

Blessed are they who possess tact! Let them rejoice and be glad in the possession of an inestimable gift, and let those who have it not bend all their energies to its acquisition.

Tact is one of the greatest aids to success in life. As a friend-winner and business-getter it is invaluable. One prominent business man puts tact at the head of the list in his success recipe, the other three things being; enthusiasm, knowledge of business, dress.

I know a man who solicits subscriptions for a periodical, who has such an exquisite way of ingratiating himself into others' favor that he gets nine subscriptions, on an average, out of every ten people he solicits. His tactful approach has won you over before you realize

TACT AS A BUSINESS-GETTER   49

it, and it is much harder for you to refuse even the thing you do not want than to take it.

Tact enables you to pass sentinels, gates and bars, gain an entrance to the very sanctum sanctorum where the tactless man never enters. Tact gets a hearing where genius cannot; it is admitted when talent is denied; it is listened to when ability without it cannot get a hearing.

As "every fish has its fly," so every person can be reached, no matter how odd, peculiar or cranky by the one who has tact enough to touch him in the right place.

What is this miracle worker called Tact?

Tact is variously defined as "Peculiar skill or adroitness in doing or saying exactly that which is required by or is suited to the circumstances"; "It is the gift of bringing into action all the mental powers in the nick of time"; "It is a combination of quickness, firmness, readiness, good-nature and facility." Webster's dictionary gets at the kernel of this wonderful quality. Tact, it says, is "adroitness in managing the feelings of persons dealt with; nice perception in seeing and doing exactly what is best in the circumstances."

It is in "managing the feelings" of his cus-

50 SELLING THINGS

tomer that the tactful man scores his strongest point. It is in sensing his moods, in being able to put himself in his place that he is always equal to the situation, that he always exercises that "nice perception in seeing and doing exactly what is best in the circumstances."

One of the best means of acquiring a tactful manner is to try to put yourself in your prospect's place, and then act toward him as you would like to have some one act toward you in like circumstances.

You are very busy, troubled about a lot of things. You may be short of capital, you may have big notes coming due, business may be dull, many things may have been going wrong with you. You may have come to your office upset by domestic troubles, you may not feel well, however well you look. Perhaps yesterday was broken up by all sorts of interruptions. You started out this morning resolved to do a splendid day's work, and hoping that you would not be bothered with callers. Perhaps you do not feel like talking business. You may have a lot of things on your mind which are perplexing you, hard problems to solve; the reports of business put on your desk this

TACT AS A BUSINESS-GETTER 51

morning may have been anything but encouraging.

In fact, you feel "out of sorts" and wish you did not have to see anybody all day. You are longing for a little time to yourself to think things over, to get your bearings, when in comes a salesman's card. You do not want to see him and would give most anything to get rid of him, although there may be a possibility that he has something that you would like, but you do not want to see him at that particular time.

"Why couldn't the man have come some other time?" you ask yourself. Against your will you say: "Well, tell him to come in." You feel grouchy, grumpy, you do not even feel like greeting him pleasantly, and you growl out a "good morning."

The salesman sits down. Your whole mind is braced against him. You do not care to see him, to talk with him. Everybody braces against a salesman. He is usually put in an unfortunate position. Instead of trying to make it easy for your visitor you make it hard for him. You make no concession if you can help it. You make him fight every inch of his way for your favor.

52 SELLING THINGS

The tactful salesman sees your mood at once, and he knows he has a hard fight ahead of him; he has to win you over inch by inch. You begin to make all sorts of excuses; you do not need new stock at present, business has been dull, your shelves are loaded down with goods, and you tell him that times are bad, the outlook is anything but promising. He does not oppose or contradict you. On the contrary, he sympathizes with you; he is patient, courteous, affable, but all the time he is trying to get the thin edge of his wedge into your mind. He knows what would win him over if he were in such a mood; his wife or mother probably knows. He has to be won over; force, argument, reason, logic will not do it, only tact will do the trick.

If you have made a study of human nature, learned to size up people quickly, you will sense a prospect's mood, even though he should try to conceal it, and you will have no difficulty in imagining yourself in his place. He has the same human qualities and the same fundamental passions as yourself. You must always be ready to pour oil on his wounds, not vinegar.

TACT AS A BUSINESS-GETTER   53

A salesman must not only use all his resourcefulness in business logic, but he must bring into play all his powers of pleasing. He should always come to his customers in a cheerful mood. No matter how upset he feels; no matter what unfortunate news he has had in the morning's mail about his sick wife, or the children lying almost at death's door, he must not show any sign of his troubles. A salesman may be in just as unfortunate a plight as his customer is, and even worse, yet he is forced to hide his feelings, and must try to "make good" under all circumstances.

The tactful salesman is "all things to all men." Not that he is deceitful or insincere, but he understands different temperaments, different dispositions, different moods, and readily adapts himself to all. He keeps his finger on the mental pulse of his prospect, and keeps track of his mental attitude. He knows, for instance, that the moment a prospect shows signs of being bored the salesman should quit, and try later, or otherwise he will prejudice his case fatally, so that the next time he calls this bored suggestion will come to the mind of the prospect, who will refuse to see him.

I was recently talking with a man who said that a salesman who did not know his business had just taken a half hour of his valuable time, trying to sell him a bill of goods that he really did not want. He said the man did not know enough to see that he was making no impression, that he was not convincing him. And although he took out his watch several times, turned around nervously in his chair, kept taking up letters from his desk, making all sorts of hints and suggestions for the salesman to get out, yet he still kept on trying to make a sale. The only redeeming quality about him, he said, was his persistency.

Now, ill-timed persistency is simply lack of tact; there is nothing praiseworthy in it. You should be able to tell by the look in your prospect's eye whether you are really interesting him or not, and if you are not you cannot convince him that he needs what you have to sell.

Getting solid with a prospect, making a favorable impression upon him, unlocking his mind, is very much like making love to a girl. You cannot browbeat, you cannot be arbitrary or disagreeable; only the gentle, attractive, tactful methods will win. The least little slip

TACT AS A BUSINESS-GETTER 55

on your part may close the door forever. No force will answer, it is all a matter of attraction and conviction. No level-headed man is going to buy until he is convinced, and tact is the most powerful convincer in the world.

Tact is never offensive. It is always a balm, allaying suspicion, and soothing and pleasing. It is appreciative. It is plausible without being dishonest, apparently consults the welfare of the second party and does not manifest any selfishness. It is never antagonistic; it never opposes, never strokes the fur the wrong way, and never irritates.

Little seven-by-nine salesmen are constantly putting stumbling blocks in their own path. They are always "putting their foot in it." They persist when persistency is ill timed. They make some unfortunate remark or allusion. They are not good students of human nature; they put up a poor sort of an argument, the same sort of talk to every man, to men of different prejudices, different ages, different dispositions. In other words, they are not tactful, and they are all the time tripping themselves up, getting into snarls, and making blunders which lose them business.

SELLING THINGS

Some one says: "The kindly element of humor almost always enters into the use of tact, and sweetens its mild coercion. We cannot help smiling, oftentimes, at the deft way in which we have been induced to do what we afterwards recognized as altogether right and best." There need be no deception in the use of tact, only such a presentation of rightful inducements as shall most effectively appeal to a hesitating mind.

A public school teacher reproved a little eight-year-old Irish boy for some mischief. The boy was about to deny the fault when the teacher said, "I saw you, Jerry." "Yes," replied the boy as quick as a flash, "I tells them there ain't much you don't see with them purty black eyes of yours." The native wit of that youngster would make him a good salesman. We do not know whether it appeased the teacher, but it certainly showed a readiness to size up and deal with a delicate situation that would have done credit to an older head.

The following paragraph, in a letter which a merchant sent out to his customers, is an example of shrewd business tact:

"We should be thankful for any information

TACT AS A BUSINESS-GETTER 57

of any dissatisfaction with any former transactions with us, and we will take immediate steps to remedy it."

Think of the wealthy customers that have been driven away from big concerns, by the lack of tact on the part of a salesman. A successful business man recently told me his experience in buying a suit of clothes at one of the leading clothiers in New York City. "The salesman who waited on me," he said, "showed me various suits of all colors and styles. He did not interest me in any particular one. He distracted my attention, being plainly indifferent and showing that he did not care whether I bought or not. After spending an hour's time, I left the place in disgust. I said to myself, 'A house carrying thousands of suits, and a good salesman, should certainly sell me one suit.' I went to another house. Then the purchase became to me more than anything else a study of salesmanship, how various salesmen handle customers. The salesman at this other place gained my confidence right at the start, showed me only three suits, interested me in a particular one, showed me why I should buy that one, and within eighteen minutes' actual

SELLING THINGS

time I paid the price, and now I am enjoying the wearing of that suit."

This shows how even the best quality of merchandise will go back to the shelf unless handled by a conscientious, tactful salesman.

It is true that there are always certain customers in every large establishment who are very hard to convince. They are suspicious, and often very disagreeable and difficult to get on with, but their patronage is valuable, and every employer prizes the salesman who can handle these difficult customers, who can please them and send them away friends instead of enemies of the house.

It must be remembered that the real test of salesmanship is the ability to handle difficult customers. Most people don't realize what is best for them to buy; they can't make up their minds without the salesman's help, or they are peculiar in their nature and require tactful management.

Many women make a business of going about among the department stores, perhaps without the slightest idea of buying anything. It becomes a sort of fixed habit with them. Some of them have a chronic habit of inde-

Tact as a Business-Getter 59

cision. They will run about the stores for weeks before they make up their minds to buy a thing that they need. They are so afraid that they will see something cheaper and much better suited to their needs after they have purchased that they postpone purchasing as long as possible. If they want a pair of shoes, a dress, a hat, or some other article, they will go round all the stores in town looking, or "shopping," as they call it, before they buy.

I know of a very clever saleswoman in a big store who has marvelous skill and tact in approaching these "lookers" or "shoppers" and turning them into customers. She begins by asking if the lady has been waited upon, and if there is anything she can do for her? With a pleasant smile, in a very sweet voice, she gets into conversation with her, and before the habitual "looker" realizes it she has become a purchaser.

To know what to do, what to say, at just the right moment is capital a thousand times more valuable than money capital, for a man with rare tact will start in business without a dollar and make a greater success than the tactless man who starts with a fortune. How many

SELLING THINGS

people in this country to-day owe their success and fortune more to the possession of tact than to ability? Tact will distance ability without it every time.

A man who with a party of friends had been fishing a long time became quite disgusted because he did not get a bite when everybody else was pulling in the speckled trout. After awhile he discovered that he had no bait on his hook. He might have been fishing there yet and never have had a bite.

Everywhere in society and in the business world we find men fishing with baitless hooks. They have no use for people with fine manners. They are gruff, uncouth. They do not believe in catering to the feelings of others. They have never learned the art of baiting things. They call a spade a spade. They have no use for frills, for decorations. They believe in striking out straight from the shoulder every time, no matter what the conditions.

Many tactless people go through life trailing bare hooks and they wonder why the fish do not bite. They do not know how to adjust themselves to conditions. They are misfits. They

TACT AS A BUSINESS-GETTER   61

appear to have been fitted for some rougher sphere and to have been dropped by accident to the earth amid conditions totally unsuited to them.

The tactless salesman is a misfit. He must either learn how to bait his hook properly, or else go into some other business for which he is better fitted.

CHAPTER X

SIZING UP THE PROSPECT

The art of all arts for the leader is his ability to measure men, to weigh them, to "size them up."

A GREAT authority on salesmanship said: "Any one can call upon a prospective buyer and go away without an order." It is up to the salesman to get what he goes after. If he knows how to size people up readily, he will be far more likely to get what he goes after than the man who can not do this. The ability to read people at sight is a great business asset.

Marshall Field was an adept in character reading. He was always studying his employees and gauging their possibilities. Nothing escaped his keen eye. Even when those about him did not know that he was thinking of them, he was taking their measure at every opportunity. His ability to place men, to weigh and measure them, to detect almost at a glance their weak and their strong points, amounted to genius.

Sizing Up the Prospect 63

If General Grant had had the same ability to read politicians and to estimate men for government positions that he had for judging of military ability, he would have made a great President. Unfortunately, he was obliged to depend too much upon the advice of friends in those matters. The result was that, as President, he did not maintain the high reputation he had made as a general.

The salesman ought to make a study of his power of penetration, of his character-reading ability. He ought to make it a business to study men and the motives which actuate them.

To be an expert in reading human nature is just as valuable to a salesman as a knowledge of law is to a lawyer, or as a knowledge of medicine is to a physician. The man who can read human nature, who can "size up" a person quickly, who can arrive at an accurate estimate of character, no matter what his vocation or profession, has a great advantage over others.

The ability to read human nature is a cultivatable quality, and we have a great opportunity in this country, with its conglomerate population, to study the various types of character. It is an education in itself to form the

64 SELLING THINGS

habit of measuring, weighing, estimating the different people we meet, for in this way we are improving our own powers of observation, sharpening our perceptive faculties, improving our judgment.

The salesman who knows anything about human nature, for instance, doesn't need to be told it won't do to approach a big business man, the head of a great establishment, as one would approach a small dealer. He will follow a different method with each, according to their different standing and temperament.

No two mentalities are exactly alike, and you must approach each one through the avenue of the least resistance. One man you can approach through his fads. If he is passionately fond of music or crazy about golf; or if he is a connoisseur in art, in sculpture, or in any other line, this may give you a hint as to the right line of approach.

If you see by a man's head and face that he has a strong mentality, that he is, perhaps, "from Missouri," you must approach him through argument, through reason. You cannot approach him in the same way you would an impressionable, fat, jolly-natured

Sizing Up the Prospect 65

man. Then the man who is selfish, domineering, imperious, who thinks he knows it all, the man to whom you never can tell anything, must be handled in quite a different manner from any of these.

Some men will take a joke, others will consider it an impertinence. One man is only convinced by logical argument; another by the judicious use of flattery. The frigid mental temperament will not respond to pleasantry; nothing but cold logic will appeal to him; the expansive, good-natured man is often reached through his fad or hobby. Sometimes you get a point of contact with your prospective customer by finding that you belong to the same lodge. Of course, it is always a good thing to find out as much as possible about a man before you call on him. Such knowledge often gives a great advantage in sizing him up properly.

If you are a good reader of character, however, you get at a glance an impression of your prospect that is fairly reliable. You can tell whether you are facing a little, weazened, dried-up soul, a man who is stingy, selfish, grasping, or whether he is a man of generous

66 SELLING THINGS

impulses, magnanimous, open-minded, kind-hearted. You can tell whether he is good-natured, jolly; whether it will do to crack a joke with him, or whether he is austere and stern; whether you can approach him in an easy, friendly manner, or whether you must keep your distance and approach him with a proper sense of his dignity and importance. Even if your prospect only assumes a stiff, stand-off demeanor you must treat him as though it were perfectly natural, otherwise he will be offended.

In sizing up a man the first thing to do is to make up your mind what kind of a heart he has. If you conclude that he has a good heart, and that he is honest and above board, even though he may be cold in appearance, and may prove a bit close-fisted, you will stand a much better chance in doing business with him than you would with a man with small shifty eyes, and the earmarks of shrewd, sharp characteristics apparent in every feature and every look.

You can read a man by his facial expression much better than you can by the bumps on his head, because the muscles of the face respond

SIZING UP THE PROSPECT 67

to the passing thought and reflect the idea, the emotion, every phase of the mental state. You know how quickly a joke, something funny, is expressed in the facial muscles; how quickly they respond to any mental state—disappointment, bad news, discouragement, sorrow, anger. The muscles of the face, its varying expressions, change with the thought. In other words, the facial expression indicates the condition of a man's mind. By this you can tell whether your prospect is in a good or a bad humor, whether he is a human icicle, cold, unfeeling, or a human magnet, tender, kind, sympathetic.

Salesmen who are poor judges of human nature, who cannot size people up, often have to batter away a long time at a wrong approach when, otherwise, they could sail right into a man's mind through the right avenue. By making head study, face study, man study, an art, you can very quickly get your line of approach. Then you will not blunder and lose time in trying to set yourself right. Many a man calls upon a prospective buyer and goes away without an order because he didn't know how to size him up. He had never studied this important side of his business.

68 SELLING THINGS

Remember that if you make a wrong approach you may have hard work to get a hearing at all; your prospect may close his mind against you at the start, and you may not be able to get into it, no matter how earnestly you try, when, if you had approached him along the line of least resistance, you could have sailed right in. In fact, the man would have invited you in.

Do not be hasty in your judgment or make up your mind too quickly in sizing up people. Hold your decision in abeyance until you have read off the character hieroglyphics written on the face and person, and in the manner, for all these are significant, and each means something. In other words, read all the earmarks or character labels on a man, get in all the evidence you can before acting on your first quick impression, because a great deal depends on the accuracy of your judgment.

Every man's face is a bulletin board; it is a program of the performance going on inside, and the important thing is to learn to read it not only quickly, but accurately.

The facial expression, the attitude, the manner, the language, the look of the eye, are let-

Sizing Up the Prospect

ters of the character alphabet which spell out the man. Everything that is natural, spontaneous, unpremeditated, is indicative of certain qualities he possesses; and if the man is putting on, if he is posing, you can pierce the mask of pretense and discount it.

If you are a good reader of character, after a few minutes study you can put together the letters of the impressions you have received and spell out the sort of a man you have to deal with, for he is covered all over with tags visible to those who have learned to read them.

Some people judge character largely by a particular feature—the mouth, the chin, the eye, the nose, etc. Napoleon used to depend a great deal upon the size of a man's nose. "Give me a man with a big nose," he used to say when choosing men for important positions. A large nose is supposed to indicate great force of character. It is said that every one resembles in greater or less degree some particular animal. Many people base their reading of character on this animal clue. Look out for the fox face; beware of the wolf face, the bird-of-prey face, for it is believed that the man who bears a strong resemblance

70 SELLING THINGS

to some animal will also usually have many of that animal's characteristics.

The main point for the salesman is to get the right start in approaching the buyer. If he makes a close study of human nature he will seldom if ever make a mistake in sizing up his man.

CHAPTER XI

HOW SUGGESTION HELPS IN SELLING

The ability to influence or induce people to purchase what you have to sell is a mental art that will repay cultivation.

"Salesmanship is the art of selling to the other fellow something he needs but doesn't know it."

"A sale is a mental thing. It results from harmonizing certain mental elements which enter into all common agreements between men."

A SHARP-WITTED lawyer after successfully defending a man accused of horse-stealing, asked him in confidence, after the trial, if he were really guilty.

"Well, Mister," replied the man, "I thought at first I had took the critter, but after listening to your speech I concluded I hadn't."

The power of suggestion may be used for base and illegitimate ends or for honorable and legitimate ones. It is his suggestive power which makes the smooth, long-headed promoter dangerous. He uses it to make people buy what they do not need, or to palm off on

72 SELLING THINGS

them fraudulent or spurious goods. The victims of these unscrupulous promoters, when under the influence of a suggestive anæsthetic, will mortgage their homes, their furniture, draw their last dollar from the savings-bank, borrow every dollar they can, to obtain the thing which is made to appear so desirable that they cannot see how they can get along without it.

Now, suggestion is just as effective when used for a lawful and honorable purpose as for an unlawful and dishonorable one. One salesman succeeds where others fail, largely because of his greater suggestive power. He draws such a vivid description of the merchandise he is selling, makes it seem so very desirable, that his prospect feels he must give him an order. The salesman knows he is selling a good thing that it is to his customer's advantage to buy. The transaction is therefore of mutual benefit to both parties, the buyer as well as the seller.

Suggestion has been defined as "whatever creates or inspires thought." As a science, suggestion "shows us how to start and steer thought." The five senses are the channels which bring us impressions from without.

How Suggestion Helps in Selling 73

"An act of the will or some association of ideas" brings impressions from *within;* this latter is auto-suggestion.

Suggestion can help you to upbuild and develop yourself, to educate and train yourself in spirit, mind, and body. "In building up character a man must have spiritual and moral backing." "As a man thinketh in his heart, so is he." This is the essence of auto-suggestion. "Thought is a creative force." It is a "motive, impelling, sustaining" force. Hence, when auto-suggestion keeps thought "working in the right direction" we have a powerful backing in all our undertakings. By thinking *definitely, steadily,* and *strongly* on useful and exalted sentiments we come into the realization of our thought aspirations. Briefly, we create within what we mentally desired steadily and intently. Thus we may build our character, ever "improving, developing, and adorning." Suggestion is our "working force."

"It (suggestion) can also help you to shape the desires and direct the will of the customers you seek to influence." In the first place, we direct the will of our customers by our very personality, which has been developed through

SELLING THINGS

auto-suggestion. Then the various steps of attention, interest, desire, and, finally, resolve, in the customer, must be induced by suggestion. He must forget himself and his own senses, ultimately; or at least, he must have had all his faculties so brought into harmony with those of the salesman that he readily accepts the salesman's ideas. "If you remember that suggestion is merely the working of the subjective mental force," says Mr. Sheldon, "and if you consider that the activity of the subjective mind is in ratio to the strength and depth of the suggestion, you have a pretty clear idea of the use that may be made of suggestion in the progress of a sale."

I have heard the story of a preacher, in Washington, who told his congregation so dramatically and so convincingly that all humanity was hanging over hell by the single thread of a cobweb, that, when the climax was reached, one man, a very learned one too, was clinging frantically to a pillar.

The simple study of psychology reveals that the activities of the will must be stirred up by approaching and capturing the outlying sentinels, namely the intellect and feelings. We

How Suggestion Helps in Selling 75

get attention through the senses, increase attention to interest through the intellect, change interest to desire through the feelings, and finally, in decision we have induced the will to act. To be sure, there is no mathematical dividing line, no architecturally apparent flights of steps; nevertheless, the true salesman is perfectly conscious of the different stages of progress of the customer's mind, and he leads him easily and naturally from one to the other. The importance of this point in selling is emphasized by a writer in "Business Philosopher," who says: "It is just as reasonable to expect your prospect to reach a favorable decision without first having been brought through the three earlier stages—attention, interest and desire—as to expect water to run up hill."

A sale is a mental process, and depends largely upon the quality and the intensity of the mental suggestion, and the confidence communicated to the would-be purchaser's mind.

Suggestion is properly used in the conduct of a sale when it is unobtrusive, and in no way savors of the pompous, swaggering, hypnotic methods of the impertinent intruder. Suggestion should be "honest and well aimed." It should help the customer's mind and inspire confidence. Suggestions to the customer should have for their object "not to overcome or dethrone the will, but simply to guide and influence it." Hypnotism, consisting in dethroning a man's will, is "the complete setting aside of the objective mind." Every salesman should study psychology. He should be able to understand the mental laws by which the mind of his prospect acts, so as to be able to read his mental operations.

Character is largely made up of suggestion; life is largely based upon it. Salesmanship is pretty nearly all suggestion.

The salesman should always keep in mind this great truth,—"The greatest art is to conceal art."

Suggestion, by its very nature, is subtle, if rightly used.

The salesman who has great skill in the use of suggestion helps the mind of the customer, without making him feel that any influence is being exerted. He leads his customer to buy after the same method by which Pope suggests men should be taught:

How Suggestion Helps in Selling 77

"Men must be taught as if you taught them not,
And things unknown proposed as things forgot."

Let the customer feel that he is buying, not that you are selling to him.

Professor Hugo Münsterberg, in an article on the psychology of salesmanship, said: "If the customer knows exactly what he wants, and has made up his mind, no suggestion is needed." It is then a case of letting well enough alone. An ill-timed or negative suggestion may spoil a sale, as in the following instance.

A farmer once went to town to buy a self-binder. He looked at one binder and was so well satisfied that he was about to buy it. At this point the salesman said: "I'll tell you, this binder has given us very little trouble."

Now, this farmer wasn't looking for a binder that was going to give him even a little trouble. He had troubles of his own. That one suggestion scared him away. He went out and bought a binder from a salesman who said, "This binder has given us excellent satisfaction."

In the offices of a New York business house there is a quotation framed, which serves the purpose of a very effective suggestion. This house is in the paper business, and, naturally, they wish to impress upon all buyers the value of using good quality paper. Here is the quotation which, I am sure, has suggested to many customers the advisability of buying good quality paper: "A printer recently uttered this truth: 'Printing doesn't improve the paper any, but, for a certainty, good paper adds considerably to the appearance and worth of printing.'"

Psychology in selling is in reality only a new name for the principles which good business men, expert salesmen, have used in all times. Diplomacy, tact, cheerfulness, the good-will habit, and the suggestion of confidence—all these form an important part of business psychology.

CHAPTER XII

THE FORCE OF CHEERFUL EXPECTANCY

The habit of expecting great things of ourselves, expecting the best things to come to us, calls out the best that is in us and brings the best to us.

Anybody can get "no" for an answer. A negative attitude attracts a negative response—and most people become negative without realizing it.

If I had a school of salesmanship I would make a specialty of the philosophy of expectancy. I would never lose an opportunity of driving home this philosophy of expecting to make good. I would drive home this lesson of expecting success, expecting to win out, until it should become a dominant note in the salesman's life.

WHEN a boy I used to go trout fishing in a rough New Hampshire stream with a noted fisherman. He understood the trout and their habits; he knew where the good holes were and the rocks behind which the big trout were waiting. I would fish on one side of the stream and he on the other, and he would catch as many trout as he could carry, while I caught very few.

80 SELLING THINGS

When this man started out to fish he would say he knew that he was going to get a big string of trout. Whenever he threw in his line he expected to get a trout. I, on the other hand, had no such hope or confidence, I did not know trout and their habits as he did, and I did not expect to catch any. The consequence was I hardly ever got a bite, while the trout nearly always went to his hook.

This is just the difference between a cracker-jack salesman and a poor one. The former knows his business thoroughly and expects to succeed. He approaches his prospect with the air of a conqueror, as a man in the habit of winning. The latter is not well posted, or he fears he won't succeed. He goes to his prospect in fear and trembling, with doubt in his mind. He doesn't believe he will get an order, and, of course, he doesn't.

You should approach every prospect courageously, confidently, not only at the top of your physical condition, but also at the top of your mental condition. You positively must be hopeful, you must expect to take an order. Doubt, fear, or anxiety will queer your sale, because you will communicate whatever is in

Force of Cheerful Expectancy 81

your own mind to your prospective customer. We radiate our moods. Our doubts and fears are very contagious.

If you carry your goods in a hearse you will not sell them. Do not approach a customer with a long, sad, disappointed countenance, as though you had just returned from a funeral. Remember you are a salesman, not an undertaker. Go to him with a face filled with hope and cheer, with confidence and assurance.

If you are a winner, your whole canvass will be conducted as though you expected to change the prospect's mind before you get through with him, no matter how antagonistic he may be, or how determined at the outset not to purchase.

There is a good deal of truth in the remark, "If you cannot learn to smile, you cannot learn to sell." The best salesmen are cheerful, optimistic, hopeful. They appreciate the commercial value of a smile, of always looking pleasant. Optimism is contagious. Everybody likes a sunny soul.

I knew a young man who would not impress people as having any marked ability, and yet this young man got fifteen thousand dollars

82 SELLING THINGS

salary, and did business enough to warrant it. He had a perfect genius for making friends. People seemed to be drawn to him as naturally as iron filings are attracted to a magnet. Everywhere he went he was the center of a circle, whether on a train, in a store, or in a hotel corridor. Everybody wanted to get near him. He seemed to radiate a hearty good cheer and good-will towards everybody. There was nothing mean or narrow about him. He was generous to a fault. He was always ready to jump up and grip you by the hand and shake it as if he was really delighted to see you—and he was. There was nothing put on. He loved everybody and wanted to help them. He was in some ways not a good business man, but his customers always anticipated his visits, and would say, "Isn't it about time for Charlie to be around? It does one good to see that fellow. He is all sunshine." Everybody knew him on his Western route, which he traveled for years. The hotel clerks all liked him and they tried to give him the best room possible whenever he came, often saving one for him for days. He was always given the best seat in the dining-room and the best

FORCE OF CHEERFUL EXPECTANCY 83

waiter, and when the orders were called off in the kitchen the waiter would say, "Give me an A1 steak for Charlie, for he is such a good fellow." Wherever he went the door flew open to him. He did not have to push hard, as others do, to get in, for everybody knew that when he came it meant a good laugh and pleasant memories.

A strong determination and tenacious persistence will sometimes enable a man to become a fair salesman, even when he lacks a pleasing personality or a persuasive manner. He conquers from sheer force of continual pounding, until he wears his would-be customer out. But a pleasing personality, charm of manner, a sunny disposition, an optimistic outlook upon life, genuineness, honesty of purpose, and simplicity, when accompanied by a positive mentality and robust determination, are the qualities which win out in a big way.

Everything depends upon the attitude of mind with which you approach a difficulty. If you are cowed before you begin, if you start out with an admission of weakness, a tacit acknowledgment of your inability to meet the emergency that confronts you, you are fore-

84 SELLING THINGS

doomed to failure. Your whole attitude lacks the magnetism that attracts success.

A book agent sometimes comes into my office, and I know by the way he enters that he does not expect to make a sale. Instead of walking with his head up, with an air of confidence and assurance, he sneaks in, apologizes, and asks me to please do him the honor to give him two or three minutes of my valuable time. He has lost his first chance by making a bad impression upon me, and it takes more time than I can give him to overcome it. He is beaten before he begins.

Quite another sort of agent calls on me occasionally, and I always buy from him whether I want what he has for sale or not. He enters with such an air of modest assurance, such confidence and expectancy in his bearing; he is so cheerful and interesting, that I positively cannot turn him down. He wins at the very outset by making a good, quick impression upon me, and getting my confidence.

Dr. Frank Crane, in an article on "A Consumer's Views on Salesmanship," gives the salesmen among other valuable points, these:

"First of all, be good-natured. I here and

Force of Cheerful Expectancy 85

now confess that nine-tenths of what induces me to buy, is the ability of the seller to jolly me along. Cheerfulness and signs that you feel good, enjoy life, and are full of glee inside, are better than a letter of introduction from Mr. Rockefeller. Avoid personal intimacies. Let me talk about myself, and look interested while I am explaining, but don't speak of yourself any more than you can help. Take an ax and chop the pronoun 'I' out of your vocabulary. What do you care?—Jolly me along."

When Dr. Crane says to "jolly" him along, he does not mean that a salesman should be frivolous, or deceitful. He simply means that he ought to make a customer feel good, make him realize his importance. Show your customer that you are interested in his needs and his problems.

If you really believe in your heart, and expect, that you are going to sell, you will communicate your faith to your prospect. This faith suggestion, if vigorously backed by the magic of polite persistence, and consistent cheerfulness, will tend to produce results like itself, just as the doubt, the failure suggestion, produces a failure result.

CHAPTER XIII

THE GENTLE ART OF PERSUASION

He is great who can alter my state of mind.

EMERSON.

"Don't struggle up hill when you can work on the level."

WHEN I was editor of a big magazine I sent an assistant to interview a young man who had had most remarkable success in the life insurance business, to get from him the secret of his rapid rise.

When my assistant returned I asked him if he had succeeded in getting his interview. "No," he said, "but the insurance manager got me to take out quite a large insurance policy."

This was a triumph of the art of salesmanship. The insurance man actually made his would-be interviewer forget what he had gone after, and induced him to buy something he had not before thought of buying, yet something which, undoubtedly, it was to his advantage to buy.

THE GENTLE ART OF PERSUASION   87

Why is it that one man will so easily change our whole mental attitude and make us do voluntarily the very thing that we had no idea of doing an hour before, and thought we never could do, when another might have talked to us until doomsday about the same thing, and never changed our mind a particle regarding it? Why is it that one man will convince us that we ought to buy an article which we were sure a few minutes before that we not only did not need or desire, but under no circumstances would buy?

Because he is a past master of the gentle art of persuasion.

How little we realize what a large part persuasion plays in our life. The clergyman, the teacher, the lawyer, the business man, the salesman, the parent, each is trying to persuade, to influence, to win over others to his way of thinking, to his principles, to accept his ideas.

Some characters are so tactful, so sunny, so bright, cheerful, and attractive that they never have to force or even to request an entrance anywhere. The door is flung wide open and they are invited to enter, just as we invite beauty, loveliness and sunshine to enter our

88 SELLING THINGS

mind. Their very presence has a subtle influence in soothing and pleasing. They know how to persuade almost without uttering a word.

Of the many elements which enter into scientific salesmanship, none is more essential than that of persuasion.

A salesman often finds a would-be customer's mind absolutely opposed to his. He does not want the merchandise, or at least he thinks he does not, and is determined not to buy it. He braces himself against all possibility of persuasion, of being influenced to do what he has decided not to do. A little later, however, he cheerfully buys the article, pays for it, and feels sure he really wants it. His entire attitude has been changed by the art of persuasion, of winning over, which was all done by successive logical steps, each of which had to be taken in order, or failure would have resulted.

The first step was to get the man's attention, —otherwise the salesman could have done nothing with him. This of itself is often a difficult matter—to get the attention of a man who is determined not to look at your goods, who had

The Gentle Art of Persuasion   89

made up his mind not to buy, and is braced against you. But a good salesman does not try to persuade a man to buy until he has not only secured his attention, but also thoroughly interested him in his proposition. Then he arouses his desire to possess the thing he has for sale, and when this is done, the sale is practically over.

I was talking recently with some friends about the rapid rise of a young salesman which surprised everybody who knew him. One of my friends said that the whole secret was his marvelous power to persuade people, to change their mind, to make a prospect see things from his point of view. He said he had never before met another man who had such remarkable success in changing another's mind to his way of thinking. "And this," he added, "is the essence, the quintessence, if you will, of salesmanship—the power to make another see things as we see them."

Persuasive power, the ability to win others over to our way of thinking, our way of looking at things, is not a simple quality. It is in reality made up of many admirable qualities which have more to do with the heart than the head.

SELLING THINGS

It is one of the lovable traits of human nature, which enables one to win out in many instances where head qualities would be of no avail.

The best and most successful teachers are not always the most learned, but those who get hold of the hearts of their pupils, whose kindness, personal interest, and sympathy inspire them to do their best. The same qualities which, apart from scholarship, make the best teachers, also make the best salesmen. While education and intelligence are indispensable, it is not so much smartness, long-headedness, cunning, as the warm human heart qualities which make a salesman popular and successful.

There is a sort of hypnotic power which passes for persuasiveness, and enables a man to get orders at the outset, but it is not based on honesty, and in the long run seriously hurts a man's business.

A magnetic, spellbinding salesman will often bring to his house larger orders than some other salesman, but in the end will lose customers and injure himself and his concern, while the one who does not sell nearly as much to start with will make many more friends, and will hold his customers, because he looks out

THE GENTLE ART OF PERSUASION 91

for their interest, and only tries to sell them what is to their advantage to buy. He will not work off a large bill of goods upon them which he knows in his heart they should not buy. He studies their needs, and so wins their confidence and good-will.

The ability to make others think as you do is a tremendous power, and carries great responsibility. If it is not kindly and honestly used it will prove a boomerang and injure most the one who uses it. He will soon become known as a "spellbinder," and people will not do business with him.

Mere "palaver and soft soap" do not cut nearly so much of a figure in salesmanship as formerly. The time has gone by forever when a salesman is chiefly measured by his ability to tell good yarns and crack jokes with his prospects. Honesty first, is the business slogan to-day. Spellbinding methods are not in demand. While you may, and should, be as affable as you please, you must be thoroughly sincere.

Even in trying to approach a man through his hobby, great caution must be used. If he is a shrewd, long-headed man he is going to see

92 SELLING THINGS

through any subterfuge, and if he gets the slightest idea that you are trying to "string" him, or if he sees the slightest evidence of insincerity or cunning, if he sees any plot back of your eye, your game is up. We must first believe in a man's integrity, even though he may deceive us, before he can persuade us to do what we thought we would not do.

To-day it is the clean, straight-from-the-shoulder talk, cold facts that the average business man wants. Yet the men of persuasive powers can present those facts in such a way that the prospect will be made to feel that the salesman is his friend and acting entirely in his interest. No man relishes the idea of being "managed," and, no matter how much he loves flattery, he will question your motive if you attempt it.

Very tactful and just praise, however, will help your cause considerably with the average man. Remember that your prospect will be always on his guard against any sort of deceit. He will be looking for evidences of insincerity. He has no intention of allowing himself to be duped or gulled. Above all, remember that there is no substitute for sincerity in any field.

The Gentle Art of Persuasion 93

There is nothing that will take the place in our lives of absolute transparency, simplicity, honesty, kindness. The Golden Rule is the only rule of conduct that will bring true success in any business.

CHAPTER XIV

HELPING THE CUSTOMER TO BUY

Satisfied customers are a perpetual lip-to-lip advertisement.

"Help your customer to buy. Don't merely sell to him."

A QUAKER merchant who had made a fortune in Liverpool, when asked how he had made it, replied, "By a single article of trade in which every one may deal who pleases—civility."

This self-same "article of trade" has been the making of the celebrated Bon Marché in Paris. The clerks in this famous establishment are instructed to show people, whether customers or not, every possible consideration. Strangers in Paris are invited to visit the Bon Marché, and are taken in hand the moment they enter the store by those who can speak their language, are shown over the whole place, and every possible attention paid to them, without the slightest influence being brought upon them to purchase. A similar courtesy is

94

HELPING THE CUSTOMER TO BUY 95

shown visitors in many well-known American concerns.

It is the service we are not obliged to give that people value most. Everybody knows that the salesman is supposed, at least, to treat a customer decently; but the over-plus of service, the extra courtesy and kindness, the spirit of accommodation, the desire to be obliging, the patience and helpfulness in trying to render the greatest possible service—these are the things customers appreciate most highly, and these are just the things that tie customers to certain houses.

Whether you are a traveling salesman or selling things behind a counter, nothing will add more to your success than the practice of that helpful courtesy which is dictated by the heart rather than the head, or by mere convention.

Doing a customer a good turn has proved the turning point in many a career. Nothing will make such a good impression upon an employer as the courtesy of an employee who has so ingratiated himself into the hearts of his customers, and so endeared himself to them, that they will always seek him out and wait to buy

SELLING THINGS

from him even at great inconvenience to themselves. Every employer knows that a clerk who attracts trade is worth ten times as much as one who drives it away.

It is said that when John Wanamaker went into business, he paid a salesman thirteen hundred dollars the first year, which was equal to all the rest of his capital. He did this because of the man's wonderful personality, his ability to attract trade, to please and hold customers so that they would come again.

I know a man who has built up a big business largely because he is always trying to accommodate his customers, to save them expense, or to assist them in buying things which he does not carry.

To-day our large business houses make a great point of pleasing customers, of obliging them and catering to their comfort in every possible way. Waiting-rooms, reading-rooms, with stationery, attendants, and even music and other forms of entertainment, are furnished by many of them.

There is a premium everywhere upon courtesy and good manners. They are taken into consideration in hiring employees just as much

Helping the Customer to Buy   97

as general ability. Great business firms find it is impossible to carry on extensive trade without the practice of courtesy, and they vie with one another in securing the most affable, and most obliging employees possible in all departments. They look upon their employees as ambassadors representing them in their business. They know that they cannot afford to have their interests jeopardized by objectionable, indifferent clerks. They know that it will not pay to build attractive stores, to advertise and display their goods, to do everything possible to bring customers to them, and then have them turned away by disagreeable, repellent clerks.

Many young men going into business seem to think that price and quality are the only elements that enter into competition. There may be a score of other reasons why customers flock to one store and pass by a dozen half-empty stores on their way. Many people never learn to depend upon themselves in their buying. They do not trust their own judgment, but depend upon the clerk who waits on them. A clerk who knows his business can assist a customer wonderfully in a very delicate way, by suggestion, by his knowledge of goods, of qualities, of fabrics, of durability.

The courtesy and affability of clerks in one store pull thousands of customers right past the doors of rival establishments where the clerks are not so agreeable or accommodating. Everybody appreciates courtesy and an obliging disposition, and a personal interest goes a great way in attracting and holding customers. Most of us are willing to put ourselves to some trouble to patronize those who show a disposition to help us, to render us real service.

What is true in regard to the man or woman who sells in a store applies with equal or even greater force to the man who goes on the road to sell.

The motto of a well-known salesman, "Help your customer to buy, don't merely sell to him," is one that it would pay every salesman to adopt. Put yourself in your customer's place, help him with your knowledge of what he really needs; mix sympathy, kindliness, helpfulness with your sales; you can give him a lot of valuable points. You are traveling all the time and constantly coming in contact with new ideas; give him suggestions from other merchants in his line.

HELPING THE CUSTOMER TO BUY   99

A wide-awake, progressive salesman, without violating confidences, can help his customers wonderfully by keeping them posted on what his competitors are doing, on the latest ideas in his line, the new and original methods. You may know of some novel and striking methods of reaching the public, of displaying merchandise and arranging store windows, or of reaching customers through unique local advertising. Give your customer every suggestion you can. You may see that he is a good business man in many respects, but seriously lacks something which you could help him to supply. If he finds you are always trying to help him, that every time you come round you give him some good suggestions, it will be pretty hard for your competitor to get his order. He will prize a man who gives him helpful suggestions.

For instance, a salesman I know, who travels for a cutlery and hardware concern, makes a specialty of keeping his customers posted as to the arrangement of goods to the best advantage in window display. He keeps track of the latest ideas, new wrinkles in his line, and gives his customers the benefit of them. If he

100 SELLING THINGS

sees that any of them are getting into ruts, or that they do not have good business systems, very tactfully, without offending them, he suggests certain new devices, say, for saving expense, little short-cuts in business methods, new ideas in filing cabinets, or some other labor or time-saving device which it will be to their advantage to adopt. In his kindly, unobtrusive way the man binds his customers to him by bands of steel so that no other salesman would have any show whatever in getting them away from him. He has built up such a large patronage for his house that rival houses have made him most tempting offers for his services.

The extra service for which he is not paid does more in helping this man to get and hold customers than the actual routine for which he receives his salary. Business men who are at a distance from the big centers of trade fully realize what this extra service means to them, and are glad to keep in touch with a helpful, up-to-date salesman.

I know a successful merchant who is so afraid that his business will get into a rut, that his standards will deteriorate through familiarity

Helping the Customer to Buy 101

with his surroundings, that every little while he invites friends to go all through his establishment in order to get the advantage of their fresh impressions, their criticisms and suggestions.

The salesman should always remember that he has an opportunity to pick up a great many new, progressive ideas which customers, who are closely confined to their business or who do not have the time to go about much, would not be likely to know about, and he can render them, as well as himself, a very great service by keeping them posted and up-to-date. Traveling salesmen are also traveling business teachers.

I know of no one quality which will help a salesman so much as an obliging spirit, the desire to be helpful, to accommodate, and to assist buyers.

Large jobbing concerns are finding that it is to their own interest to look after the interests of their customers, to aid them in every possible way, such as suggesting attractive ways of advertising, giving them new ideas and suggestions as to the best arrangement of their merchandise and advising them on other important points.

102 SELLING THINGS

Many large concerns aid their customers financially. Mr. H. N. Higinbotham, Marshall Field's well-known credit man, was noted for helping customers, especially when they were financially embarrassed. He often assisted them to get mortgages and loans, and, in fact, frequently made personal loans to the customers of his house. Of course affairs of this sort must go to the credit man, but at the same time a salesman often leads up to them, and thus relieves the embarrassment of customers.

Some time ago a manager of a large concern told me that he helped a customer to get a thirty-thousand-dollar mortgage on his property, an accommodation he was not able to get at the bank on a strictly business basis. Many small houses, especially in the West, have come to look upon the jobbing and wholesale houses they trade with as real friends, and whenever they are hard pushed for money they are the first places they go to for help.

Hundreds of Western concerns, through the initiative of the salesman, owe their prosperity to-day to the assistance of the jobbing house which carried them through hard times.

Helping Customer to Buy   103

When they could not have secured the ready cash they needed upon purely business grounds, firms accommodated through the efforts of a salesman become life customers and a perpetual advertisement for the concern which has helped them, always saying a good word for it whenever possible.

There are a hundred and one small ways in which both wholesale and retail salesmen can accommodate their trade. Be alert to do all these trifling personal favors, which mean so much and cost only a little thoughtfulness.

A word of caution in regard to promises. Guard carefully against making promises you can't fulfill. In your zeal to help the customer do not, for instance, promise deliveries that are next to impossible or very hard for your house. You thereby hurt yourself, your customer and your firm. Be accommodating, but always use common sense.

Your customer may forget a lot of things which you say to him, but he will not forget how you spent your time and energy in trying to show him that which would be a real benefit to him; your effort to give him new ideas, to show him how he could be a little more up-to-date;

104 SELLING THINGS

your explaining to him how other progressive men in his own line were doing things. There is nothing which makes a better impression on a man or woman than the unselfish effort to please, to be of service, and the demand for salesmen and all sorts of employees who will put themselves out to do this is constantly growing. There was a time when human hogs could do business, provided they had the goods and could deliver them, but all this has changed; to-day the art of getting on in the world is largely the art of pleasing.

CHAPTER XV

CLOSING THE DEAL

Don't talk yourself out of a deal.

There are many men trying to sell merchandise who are almost salesmen. They seem to have about every qualification excepting the ability to close a sale.

"Brevity is the soul of wit."

A MAN who was waiting impatiently outside the church for his family, asked the janitor if the pastor was not through with his sermon. "Yes," said the janitor, "he is through, but he hasn't stopped yet."

Many a salesman queers a sale by not stopping when he is through—his tongue outlasts his brain. He has not tact enough to see that when he has convinced his prospect it is time to close the deal. Others again make the mistake of lingering after their object is accomplished, squandering their own and their prospect's time to no purpose.

If there is anything a business man appreciates in a caller it is a regard for the value of

106 Selling Things

his time. Every minute is precious with a busy man, and directness, conciseness of statement, saying a lot in a few words, always makes a favorable impression.

"When you get what you went after, quit," said one big selling agent of a national concern. "Many a sale has been queered because the salesman 'stuck ground' after he had signed his man."

"I knew a salesman who put over a big deal one afternoon. Then he lighted a cigar and sat talking with the man to whom he had sold. Presently the telephone rang. It was a long-distance call from the buyer's financial headquarters. Evidently the president of the concern was advising his representative to economize, to cut expenses everywhere he could, to lay off men, and to buy only necessities.

"I'm glad you didn't go," said the buyer to the salesman, after he had hung up the receiver; "I find my appropriation has been decreased and I won't be able to take those goods now. This saves my writing you to cancel the order."

"That salesman always said he talked himself out of that deal. He felt sure that if he had not been there, the buyer would have kept

CLOSING THE DEAL 107

the goods and would have started his economy on the next salesman."

Some salesmen with many splendid qualities talk themselves out of business. They tire out their prospect, bore him, disgust him. They do not have tact enough to see that when a prospect begins to move about uneasily in his chair and to look around the room that he wishes they would get out. Now, when a man feels pressed for time, or when you no longer interest him, it is a great mistake to try to hold him or to recover his lost interest. It is high time to stop and close the deal.

Brevity and directness are the very soul of business, and make a good impression on a business man. The roundabout talker, the man who prefaces everything with a long introduction, the man who goes around and around half a dozen times before he gets to the point, tires and irritates a busy man. Good business men are direct. They drive right to the marrow of things at the first plunge; and when a deal is put through, they want to close and go on to the next thing.

The closing step is one of the most important in any business transaction. There

108 SELLING THINGS

are plenty of salesmen who can conduct the progress of a sale clear up to the point of closing the deal quite as well as infinitely better salesmen, but here they fall down. They cannot gather up their threads of persuasive argument and reasoning to make a successful close, and when they become panicky they communicate their fear to the coveted customer, and then the game is up.

Like all other points of salesmanship, the quickest and the simplest way of taking the final step is the best. Closing a deal is the result of having created an earnest wish on the part of the customer for what you have to sell. He must have the "I want it" feeling or you are likely to have trouble. If you have made your customer *want* your goods, made him see the profit and the pleasure that will accrue to him in buying, then the question of closing the deal becomes very much simplified.

There is a school of experts strongly inclined to what they call "Reason Why" advertising. I think the "Reason Why" school is strongly entrenched. We buy things because there are reasons why we should buy them, and the salesman who can set forth the strongest reasons

Closing the Deal

why, will have the least trouble in closing his deals. The goods may be all right in themselves, but the sale will not be made unless you can make the customer see why he, personally, should buy.

A shrewd salesman will let his prospect or customer handle the samples as much as possible, and let him do the talking. You watch him. You will learn a great deal about the operation of the man's mind. If he shrugs his shoulders and shakes his head when he picks up a particular sample you had better not talk too much about that; it will not pay to try to convince him; you had better try something else, at least for the moment. If you see that he is anxious to make an impression upon you by his skill and his knowledge of goods, don't try to switch him to something else. If he expresses an admiration for a certain piece of goods follow it up. If it is regarding the color, or shade, do not go too much into the quality of the texture. Let him take the lead.

In closing, always look for a peaceful and cheerful surrender of the will. If the standards of the house are high, and if the goods are

110 SELLING THINGS

of a high quality, the customer will feel quite reassured in surrendering his will to that of the salesman. He really thinks his will is deciding. Very often he is right, but it is the duty of the salesman to guide the will of the customer, so that the right decision will be made with the least loss of time and energy.

The "winner" salesman does not wait for his prospect to say, "You can put me down for so and so. Yes, I'll take that." He uses his own positive mind to guide and bring to a focus the vacillating, almost-decided mind of the prospect, for he knows from experience that the temptation of most buyers is to hang off, to wait. Knowing the processes through which his prospect's mind is passing, he seizes upon the psychological moment to close up the thing, to bring the man's mind to a decision.

Always be ready to close. Have plenty of *well-sharpened* pencils, a fountain pen in *good working order, clean* order blanks, and every facility at hand for signing orders. The customer should not be expected to fill in name, facts or figures any more than is absolutely necessary. When asked to sign his name, the salesman should indicate clearly the exact line

CLOSING THE DEAL 111

on which the name should be written. The idea is to make everything so simple and easy that the mind of the customer does not have a chance to balk. Human nature is peculiar. Very often men are contrary. They will act against their own best interests, just because they think some one is trying to compel them to do a particular thing. We all love freedom.

In closing a deal, have all minor points made clear, such as time of delivery, method of packing, method of delivery, the way payment is to be made, and all similar details.

CHAPTER XVI

THE GREATEST SALESMAN—ENTHUSIASM

"What are hardships, ridicule, persecution, toil, sickness, to a soul throbbing with an overmastering enthusiasm?"

Enthusiasm is the best salesman. Cultivate it; it is contagious.

You can't built a fire with the fuel all wet.

WHY is it that one salesman can often accomplish three or four times as much as another? The difference is not always that of ability. It is often a difference in the effort—in the character of the effort. One salesman tries harder. He adds enthusiasm and a splendid zest to his work, which increases the quality as well as the quantity of the result.

Joyous zeal, dead-in-earnestness, will sell more goods than all the technical training in the world, minus enthusiasm.

How often have I heard salesmen say in the morning that they fairly dreaded the day's work, that the hours dragged and that they

THE GREATEST SALESMAN 113

were glad when the ordeal was over. They felt no enthusiasm for their employment.

Can any one hope to succeed in life who considers a day's work an ordeal, who goes to it as a slave lashed to his task?

An employer measures his employees largely by the spirit in which they do their work. The salesman who goes to his task with energy, determination, and enthusiasm, by his very bearing gives assurance that the thing he undertakes will not only be done, but will be done as well as it can be done. On the other hand, when a salesman drags himself about as though existence were a burden, when he takes hold of his work with repugnance, as though he dreaded it, it does not take an expert judge of human nature to know that he will never amount to anything.

No matter how strongly and perfectly constructed, or how powerful a locomotive may be, unless the water is heated to two hundred and twelve degrees, the train will not move an inch. Warm water, water at two hundred and eleven degrees will not answer. The water must be at the boiling point.

No matter how fine a brain or how good an

114 SELLING THINGS

education a salesman may have, without the steam of enthusiasm, which propels the human machine, his work will be ineffective. It is the enthusiastic man in every trade or profession, the man with fire and iron in his blood, whose enthusiasm is at the boiling point, who makes things move in this world. The half-hearted, indifferent, aimless worker, who is never aroused to the two-hundred-and-twelve degree of live interest and enthusiasm in his especial task, is headed for failure. He will never be his own manager. He is lucky if he succeeds in holding down even a poor job.

The prizes of life are for the dead-in-earnest and enthusiastic. The world has ever made way for enthusiasm. It compels men to listen. It convinces the most skeptical. As Bulwer-Lytton once said: "Nothing is so contagious as enthusiasm; it is a real allegory of the Lute of Orpheus; it moves stones; it charms brutes. Enthusiasm is the genius of sincerity; and truth accomplishes no victories without it."

Knowledge and skill have never been a match for enthusiasm. It multiplies a man's power, raises whatever ability he has to its highest. One talent with enthusiasm back of it has ever

THE GREATEST SALESMAN 115

accomplished more than ten talents without it. Enthusiasm is the powder that drives the bullet home to its mark.

To produce the best results, enthusiasm must be steady, continuous, not fitful or uncertain.

I know a man who is a valuable solicitor if his employers can only keep him keyed up to the right point, supplied with enthusiasm. When his enthusiasm is at high tide he accomplishes wonders, but the moment it ebbs he is good for nothing. And his enthusiasm often ebbs; it is very uncertain. One day he will impress you as a powerful man, a man with great determination, vigor and push—he makes everything move; then you meet him on one of his off days, when the tide is out, and scarcely know him. His mentality is flabby, his courage is down. He goes about with a blue and discouraged look, and is practically good for nothing. But when he rallies and his courage and enthusiasm come back, he is a regular giant.

If this man would learn to control his moods and get complete possession of himself; if he would strengthen his will so that he should always be ruler in his mental kingdom, instead

116 SELLING THINGS

of abdicating every now and then and allowing his pessimism, his blue moods to take control and rule him, he would be invaluable—a king in his line.

Enthusiasm must be guided by level-headedness or it may defeat its object. Some people allow their enthusiasm to run away with them and thus greatly weaken their power and possibilities. While it is an indispensable factor in salesmanship, too much enthusiasm develops weakness, destroys one's good sense and good judgment and one's ability to convince people. And the power of carrying conviction to the mind of a prospective buyer is the very marrow of salesmanship.

I have known over-enthusiastic young salesmen to be so completely carried away with the possibilities of what they were selling, to exhibit so little judgment and so much fervor in their canvass, that they aroused suspicion in the minds of their prospects as to their good judgment.

In cases of this sort a level-headed man will say to himself: "This young fellow is too wrought up over this article; he is hypnotized by it and has an exaggerated idea of its merits.

THE GREATEST SALESMAN 117

No man in this state of mind is reliable; his judgment is warped. He is honest enough, but I cannot afford to rely on what he says. He is too enthused to be trustworthy."

You can be as enthusiastic as you please without overstepping the bounds of reason. The A1 salesman knows how to steer his course between the enthusiasm that excites suspicion, arouses distrust, and the enthusiasm that persuades and convinces. There is now and then one who with abounding enthusiasm, guided by good judgment and horse-sense, pours his very life into his sale, just as a great advocate flings his life into his pleading. He is the sort of man who will win out in any proposition he attempts to put through.

On the other hand, there are lukewarm salesmen who put so little of themselves into their sale, so little enthusiasm and zest, so little magnetism, so little diplomacy and tact, and so little of the art of persuasion, that they remain third or fourth rate all their lives. They barely get a living in a field where the energetic, enthusiastic man makes a fortune.

The salesman or other worker who gives only his second best instead of his best, who

118 SELLING THINGS

gives indifference instead of enthusiasm, who doesn't think it worth while to fling his soul into his work, never amounts to much. In an age when increasing stress is everywhere placed on efficieney, and yet more efficiency, there is no future for the indifferent. Give to the world the best you have and the best will come back to you.

CHAPTER XVII

THE MAN AT THE OTHER END OF THE BARGAIN

A Golden Rule for every salesman: "Put yourself in your customer's place."

When you are in doubt as to how your acts will affect another, you must ask yourself this question, "Would I like to have some one else do this to me?"

NATHAN STRAUSS, when asked what had contributed most to the success of his remarkable career, replied, "I always looked out for the man at the other end of the bargain." He said that if he got a bad bargain himself he could stand it, even if his losses were heavy, but he could never afford to have the man who dealt with him get a bad bargain.

There is no one thing that has so much to do with a business man's success as the absolute confidence of the public. Confidence has everything to do with patronage. We like to patronize the firm which has a good reputation, and many prefer to pay more for articles in a

120 SELLING THINGS

reliable store that guarantees their quality than to buy similar articles at a much lower price in an unreliable store. People are afraid to go into unreliable places. They have a feeling that they will be swindled in some way; that the lower price only covers up poor quality.

You may bring customers to your store once by shrewd schemes and advertising, but you cannot hold them by this means alone. Unless you satisfy them, give them good value for their money, you cannot induce them to come again. But the satisfied customer is a perpetual advertisement. He not only comes again, but he sends his friends, and they furnish a perpetual lip-to-lip advertisement which gives stability and permanence to a business.

The man who thinks he is going to make a fortune without considering the man at the other end of the bargain is very short-sighted. In the long run, the customer's best good is the seller's best good also; and, other things equal, the man succeeds best who satisfies his customers best, who gains their confidence, so that they will not only come back, but always bring others with them. In the same way, the ideal

The Man at the Other End   121

salesman must impress his customers with his honesty, sincerity and frankness. He must be shrewd and sagacious without being deceptive. Trickiness, dishonest methods, may procure a man's orders at the start, but before long he will find that in selling goods, as in everything else, honesty is the best policy.

A little while ago I heard a salesman say to a friend, "I don't care whether a man sells my goods or not, I sell him every dollar's worth I can, just the same. If he is overstocking the store, that is his business. I push my sales just as far as I can."

Now, when this young salesman's customers find that out, as, sooner or later, they will, they will distrust him. They will be on their guard against him, and ultimately he will lose their patronage.

Remember, Mr. Brilliant Salesman, that stuffed, forced orders are dangerous. They are boomerangs. When, by hypnotic over-persuasion, you work off goods upon a customer which he does not need, you are likely to hear from him again. The profits of a single such sale have often lost a salesman the profits of a life customer. There is nothing so disas-

122 SELLING THINGS

trous as a disappointed or a deceived customer.

Many people are beguiled into buying what they do not need and cannot afford, because they do not know how to protect themselves from the expertness or hypnotism of unprincipled salesmen. Especially is this true of colored people in the South, whose simple, untrained minds are the easy victims of the smooth oily promoter or salesman.

I have known of negro families who did not have a whole plate, or a knife and fork in the house, to buy from unscrupulous agents plush autograph albums, books which they could not read or understand, pictures, picture frames, organs, pianos, etc., when they were so poor that every member of the family was ragged, and apparently only half nourished.

Many such agents and solicitors, who travel through the country, live upon the gullibility of people who are not mentally equipped to protect themselves against their dishonest wiles.

Every salesman is familiar with the "tricks of the trade" which the unscrupulous practice, but to which the conscientious man will not resort. His clean record, his straightforward methods, his reputation for reliability, mean in-

The Man at the Other End 123

finitely more to him than to get an order by driving a sharp bargain, deceiving, taking advantage of, or hypnotizing his customer. His honesty, his character, is dearer to him than any gain, temporary or permanent, however great.

Nor is there any great demand for the man whose sole aim is to "deliver the goods," regardless of the methods employed. They may be hired by cheap-John concerns which have no reputation to sustain, but high-class houses will have nothing to do with them. They know very well that men who practice real dishonesty in their mental methods, who use unfair means in winning confidence, only to abuse it, who make a business of overcoming weak minds for the purpose of deceiving them—they know that such men would hurt their house, injure their reputation. They know very well that the tricky, dishonest man who deceives or who over-sells his customer, is not a good man for his house.

The high-class salesman, like the high-class house, thinks too much of his good name, too much of his customers' good opinion of him, to attempt to practice the slightest deception

SELLING THINGS

in his dealings with them. Their implicit faith in him, their belief that they can absolutely depend upon what he tells them, that it will not be the near-truth, but the exact truth, his real desire to serve them, these things mean infinitely more to him than the taking of an order. His reputation for straightforwardness, for reliability, his reputation as a man, is his chief capital. He is doing business without money; his only assets are his ability and his character, and he cannot afford to throw these away or vitiate them by dishonest mental practices.

Aside from the vital question of character, he is a very poor salesman who does not study the interest of the man at the other end of the bargain.

CHAPTER XVIII

MEETING AND FORESTALLING OBJECTIONS

Opposition is the physical culture of determination.

You must have the courage of your convictions, and if you have theories you should be able to put them to a practical test.

Don't canvass too much with your legs—use your brains.

THERE are two kinds of objections which are met by all salesmen—valid and invalid. Naturally, it is impossible to overcome valid objections. It would be a mistake on the part of the salesman to try to overcome them. The important thing is for him to recognize that they are valid, and to abide by the decision of the prospective customer.

Very frequently, however, what appear on the surface to be valid objections, are merely excuses. Never accept an excuse as a real objection. Do not come out bluntly and tell the customer that he is merely making an excuse, or that he is hedging, but, rather, switch

126 SELLING THINGS

the selling talk on to a little different track, so that he will see there is no real, good reason for the stand he is taking.

It is not so easy to meet such objections as—"The goods are not suitable for our needs,"—"The price is exorbitant," or "We cannot afford to buy now." But in some cases, objections of this sort may not be really valid; often they are merely excuses to put off buying. Here is where the salesman must show his power of reasoning and persuasion. He should make clear to the customer that, at first thought, these may seem to be valid objections, but that, in reality, if he will only think of such and such points and reasons, he will see, after all, he should buy.

No doubt there is far more trouble constantly arising on this score than there should, because the salesman cannot gently guide the mind of the customer to where all objections are forgotten. It is human nature to object, find fault, and pick flaws, and the salesman must be prepared both for the real or valid, and for the unreal, or invalid objections. Above all he must be prepared beforehand to answer, and to answer clearly and logically,

FORESTALLING OBJECTIONS 127

the many very common objections which are brought up in connection with his line of goods.

The older, more experienced salesmen and the sales managers, usually, have thought out the most effective answers to the objections that are ordinarily made. The young inexperienced salesman must go to them for advice. He must be posted, if possible at the start, on the right answers to, let us say, the ten most ordinary objections that are heard in his line of business.

One of the most successful life insurance managers in the United States has given to his men a standard answer to this very common objection, met by salesmen when trying to sell life insurance,—"I would like to take the matter up with my wife."

The salesman is taught to use the law of non-resistance, and to say: "That's a very good idea, Mr. Blank. This is such an important matter you certainly ought to have your wife's opinion about it; but, allow me to suggest that before you take the matter up with her, it would be best to have our doctor examine you, to make sure that you can pass the physical examination, because, if you told your wife

128 SELLING THINGS

that you were going to take life insurance, and you then failed to pass the examination, she would be very much worried about you as long as she lives." The prospect will, almost invariably, say—"Yes, you're right about that—I think I ought to take that precaution." It is needless to say that nine times out of ten, after the doctor has made the examination, it is quite easy to close the sale, whereas it would have been impossible, or very difficult, had the matter first been taken up at home, and a lot of objections brought up in the absence of the salesman.

Some say that you should never risk antagonizing a customer by departing from the law of non-resistance. Ordinarily, this is sound logic; but just as there are exceptions to every rule, so there are certain types of men, with whom at least *seeming opposition* or an attitude of "take it or leave it" will be most effective.

There are men and moods and times when only a good knowledge of human nature and a thorough sizing up of a customer will enable the salesman to get what he goes after. Also there are occasions when the most expert salesman will meet at least temporary defeat.

FORESTALLING OBJECTIONS 129

By the time you have exchanged a few sentences with your prospect, you can size him up fairly well and can get a pretty good idea of what you are up against, and how difficult a task is before you in order to interest him, to change his thought, to neutralize his natural prejudice against every one who has anything to sell, and against you in particular. There is a natural barrier, at first, between two people who meet under such conditions, and it depends largely upon you as a man, upon your talk, your ability to open up your nature, to show the best side of yourself, the attractive, the popular, magnanimous side, whether you gradually change the prospect's opposition to indifference, his indifference to interest and his interest to desire to possess what you have to sell.

You should never argue with a customer in the sense of quarreling or disputing with him, but there are times when you must reason with him, to show him he is wrong. Do not, however, make a customer feel "cheap," or humiliated, or anger him by opposition, especially in matters outside of your business.

I have in mind a salesman who had practi-

130 SELLING THINGS

cally closed a big order with a prospect when some allusion was made to the political situation. The salesman reflected upon the administration, and the prospect jumped on him with both feet and became so angered that he positively refused to give him the order.

Now, this salesman was not there to discuss politics or to convince his prospect that he was on the wrong side of any public question. He was there to sell his goods and not to talk politics.

No matter what happens never lose your head and never, under any circumstances, show resentment or disappointment or allow yourself to be drawn into an argument. There is always a temptation to have the last word, and it is of the utmost importance that you should leave a pleasing picture of your call. Otherwise when you return the association of a disagreeable experience may bar you out.

Some sales managers do not believe in paying any attention to objections. They say it is best to make the salesman so familiar with his goods, and so enthusiastic about them, that he will forestall all objections, or overcome them by ignoring them, in the sense that he will

Forestalling Objections   131

not try to answer objections if they are made, and he will not talk or act as if he expected any to be made. There is a certain amount of sound philosophy in this attitude, but it is my opinion that a salesman will have more confidence in himself, and will be better equipped for many emergencies, if he has been thoroughly coached in the most commonly met objections, by having good, sound answers right at the tip of his tongue.

Never meet objections by cutting prices.

It is the easiest thing in the world to prejudice a prospect's mind by offering to cut prices. He will think you are doing it to get his first order, and that you will make it up the next time. He is watching you with "all his eyes." His perceptive faculties are on the alert, ready to catch any unguarded word, the slightest contradiction, measuring up the improbabilities in your argument. In other words, he is trying to find holes in your proposition. It is human nature to brace up against a new salesman and to try to down him with objections. Don't destroy confidence at the start by price cutting.

Remember, objections are, generally, mere excuses. More than half the time they are not

132   SELLING THINGS

sound reasons for not buying. Therefore, do not take objections too much to heart. Know how to answer them satisfactorily, but be careful not to magnify their importance.

CHAPTER XIX

QUALITY AS A SALESMAN

Integrity is the ground of mutual confidence.

Never misrepresent your goods; when it becomes necessary to do so it is time to quit the business.

A.J. LAUVER, General Manager Burroughs' Adding Machine, says, "The ideal salesman is one who is making an honest and determined effort to render a real service to his customers. He believes thoroughly in the value of his goods and has faith in the honesty and ability of the house he represents."

An unqualified confidence in the value of what you are selling will multiply your selling ability tremendously, just as a lack of confidence in its merit will greatly diminish your power to make a sale. All of your mental operations follow confidence. Your faculties will not give out their best unless they are led by the honest faith in your house and in your goods which generates enthusiasm.

134 SELLING THINGS

The salesman communicates his faith, or lack of it, to the experienced buyer. Whatever passes through your mind will be telegraphed with lightning rapidity to your prospect's mind. He will feel what you feel. He will sense mentally what you are picturing secretly, as you imagine, in your own mind. If doubt is there, if unbelief is there, he will feel them no matter what you may say to the contrary. He can tell very quickly whether you really believe what you are saying or whether you are just talking for a sale. He can tell whether you honestly believe that what you are trying to sell would be good for him to buy or not.

The consciousness that you are representing an absolutely reliable firm, and that you are selling a superb thing, something which you really believe it would be as advantageous for your prospect to buy as it would be for you to sell, will not only increase your self-confidence, but will also lend wonderful dignity and power to your bearing and your manner, and greater force to your presentation and persuasion.

On the other hand, if you are conscious that you are selling shams, that you are merely try-

QUALITY AS A SALESMAN   135

ing to get a person to buy that which you know will not be of much value to him, you are immediately shorn of power. The conviction that you are not doing your fellow-man a good turn, that, on the contrary, you are trying to deceive him, trying to palm off on him an article which you would not buy yourself, will make you contemptible in your own eyes and also in the eyes of the man who is shrewd enough to see through you.

Nothing can take the place of confidence in the quality of what you are selling. Quality is really the best salesman in the world. The article that is a little better than others of the same kind—that is the best, even if the price is higher—"carries in its first sale the possibilities of many sales, because it makes a satisfied customer, and only a satisfied customer will come again."

The salesman thinks more of himself when he is conscious that he is giving his customer the best that can be had. The assurance that it is not possible for another to beat what he offers is a wonderful tonic and encourager to the seller. He does not need to resort to "tricks of the trade"; nor does he have to hang

136 SELLING THINGS

his head or apologize when he approaches his prospect, for he knows that he is backed by quality and that there will be no disappointment or "come backs."

A superb quality, like good things to eat, always leaves a good taste in the mouth, and the salesman who deals in the best knows that he will be welcome when he goes back for another order to a buyer who has once had a taste of the quality of his goods.

The reputation of a house noted for its square dealing is of itself a powerful salesman, and representatives of such a house have a tremendous advantage over those who represent tricky, sharp-dealing, shoddy houses, where the buyer knows that he has got to look out for himself, to drive a sharp bargain or get taken in—and he knows that he is liable to be taken in anyway.

Quality is the best possible advertisement. The salesmen of a house thoroughly established in the confidence of the public have a comparatively easy time of it, because they do not have to do nearly as much talking and convincing as those who represent unreliable concerns. The high reputation of a house is a great business

QUALITY AS A SALESMAN 137

asset, and a salesman's best argument. It is not so difficult a matter to persuade men to buy what they know from experience to be all that it is represented to be.

When a customer has been in the habit of buying the best, dealing with a quality house, and has acquired a taste for the best, he does not like the second-best—only the best is good enough for him.

International sales experts tell us that is where American salesmen fall down, especially in seeking foreign trade—in South America for instance. They dwell at too great length on price, and skim over quality. They dilate on cheapness, and the inference is that the goods must be low grade to be marketed at such a low price.

No matter how hard pushed you may be, never undertake to sell questionable goods; never taint your reputation, or smirch your character by becoming the representative of a shifty, dishonest concern. Resolve that whatever comes you will not cheapen yourself by stooping to low-down methods, that you will not sell shabby goods, or deal in cheap-John commodities. Resolve that you will be a high-

188 SELLING THINGS

class man or nothing, that you are not going to do another's lying for him, that you are not going to deceive for a salary, that you are not going to do anything which will make you think less of yourself, which will make you less of a man.

CHAPTER XX

A SALESMAN'S CLOTHES

The apparel oft proclaims the man,
SHAKESPEARE.

The consciousness of being well and fittingly dressed has a magic power in unlocking the tongue and increasing the power of expression.

In differentiating the essentials of success in selling, a specialty expert said: "I find that when I am in prime condition physically, and am well dressed, so that I do not have to think about myself or my clothing, I can put up a much better canvass, because I can concentrate my mind with greater force."

In a letter to his home office, a rising young salesman wrote: "To me there is a great mystery in the influence of good clothes. Somehow I think more of myself when I am conscious that I am well groomed, well dressed, and I can approach people with much more confidence.

"When I first started canvassing I tried to

140   SELLING THINGS

economize too much on my clothing. Some stormy mornings I would start out wearing shabby old clothes and without fixing up as I should, and somehow I felt cheap all day. I could not approach a prospect with the same air of victory; I did not feel quite right; I could not put up as good a canvass, and of course did not make as many sales as when I was up to the mark in clothes and general appearance.

"I thought at the start I could not afford to dress well, but I soon found that this was a very great mistake, and that a good appearance is a big asset in canvassing. I was going through college then, and, as I had to pay all of my expenses, a dollar meant a good deal to me; but I actually borrowed money to buy a good suit of clothes, and I found it paid. I felt better when I had that suit on. I could take more orders, and in a short time returned the amount I had borrowed. This influence of good clothes is a curious thing, but it is certainly a power."

Whatever one's business, it is worth while to try to ascertain as nearly as possible the paying point of your clothes. You cannot afford to go much below or above this point. In some

A Salesman's Clothes 141

cases it pays to dress superbly, right up to the mark in every detail, because people judge our business standing by our appearance, and we cannot afford to give the impression of poverty, especially if we are representing a prosperous line of business. If a man's appearance indicates lack of prosperity, people naturally get a poor impression not only of his own success, but also of the quality and success of the firm he represents.

A. T. Stewart was one of the first great merchants to appreciate the tremendous influence upon customers, especially women customers, of good-looking, well-dressed young men clerks. He would not have a clerk in his employ who did not present an attractive appearance. He knew and appreciated the importance of putting up a good front as an asset. He did not care much for human diamonds in the rough. He preferred a cheaper stone, polished, to a pure gem, unpolished.

Every progressive merchant knows that a first unfavorable impression on a customer is a costly thing. He knows that soiled collar or cuffs, a frayed tie, unpolished shoes, uncared-for finger nails, grease spots on a suit, will not

142 SELLING THINGS

only make a bad impression, but will drive away trade.

Most large business houses make it a rule not to employ any one who looks shabby or careless, who does not at least try to make a good appearance, the best his means will permit, when he applies for a position.

Neatness of dress, cleanliness of person and the manner of the applicant are the first things an employer notices in a would-be employee. If his clothes are unbrushed, his trousers baggy, his shoes unblacked, his tie shabby, his hands soiled or his hair unkempt, the employer is prejudiced at once, and he does not look beneath this repellent exterior to see whether it conceals merit or not. He is a busy man and takes it for granted that if the youth has anything in him, if he is made of the material business men want in their employ, he will keep himself in a presentable condition. At all events, he does not want to have such an unattractive looking person about his premises.

You may say that an employer ought to be a reader of real merit, real character, and that it is not fair to estimate an applicant for a position by such superficial things as the clothes

A Salesman's Clothes 143

he wears. You may also say that a customer should not allow himself to be prejudiced against a man, or the house he represents, because he is not a fine dresser. But that doesn't help matters or alter facts. We go through life tagged all over, labeled with other people's estimate of us, and it is pretty difficult to get away from that, even if it is unjust.

Say what we will, our position in life, our success, our place in the business or professional world, or in society, depends very much upon what other people think of us, and our clothes, at first especially, while we are making our way in the world, play an important part in their judgment of us. They have a great deal to do with locating us.

In a way our lives are largely influenced by other people's opinion of us, and we should not be indifferent to it. This does not mean that we cannot be independent and exercise our own will, but that we cannot afford to create a bad impression. Suppose, for example, you are a young business man and that every bank official in your town is so prejudiced against you that they will not give you credit. You need it very much, but while the fact that you

144 SELLING THINGS

know you are absolutely honest and absolutely reliable gives you great inward satisfaction, it does not give you the needed money. The prejudice of the bank officials may be unfounded, but it acts powerfully against you.

You may know perfectly well that you would make a better mayor for your town than anybody else in it, but if the majority of the voters are prejudiced against you, no matter how worthy of their confidence, you will not be elected. Whatever your business or profession the impression you create will make a tremendous difference in the degree of your success.

"Every man has a letter of credit written on his face." We are our own best advertisements, and if we appear to disadvantage in any particular we are rated accordingly.

"You cannot estimate the influence of your personal appearance upon your future. Other things equal, it is the young man who dresses well, puts up a good front, who gets the order or position, though often he may have less ability than the one who is careless in his personal appearance. Most business men regard a neat, attractive appearance as evidence of

A Salesman's Clothes 145

good mental qualities. We express ourselves first of all in our bodies. A young man who is slovenly in appearance and who neglects his bath will, as a rule, neglect his mind.

To save money at the cost of cleanliness and self-respect is the worst sort of extravagance. It is the point at which economy ceases to be a virtue and becomes a vice. In this age of competition, when the law of the survival of the fittest acts with seemingly merciless rigor, no one can afford to be indifferent to the smallest detail of dress, or manner, or appearance, that will add to his chances of making a success in life.

Remember that the world takes you largely at your own valuation; your prospective customer will be repelled or attracted by your appearance, and your clothes are as important as your bearing and manners. In fact they will to a great extent determine your bearing and manner. It has been well said that "the consciousness of clean linen is in and of itself a source of moral strength, second only to that of a clean conscience. A well ironed collar or a fresh glove has carried many a man through an emergency in which a wrinkle or a rip would

146 SELLING THINGS

have defeated him." Our clothes have a subtle mental influence from which there is no escape.

The consciousness of shabbiness, incompleteness, or slipshodness tends to destroy self-respect, to lessen energy and to detract from one's general ability.

In order to dress properly, you must study the colors and the styles that are most becoming to you, that add most to your appearance. Don't wear a profusion of rings or flashy jewelry; don't indulge in "loud" neckties or anything that would make you conspicuous. All these things make a bad impression.

An excellent rule for dress is found in the advice of Polonius to his son Laertes, when he is about to start for the royal court of France.

> "Costly thy habit as thy purse can buy
> But not express'd in fancy; rich not gaudy;
> For the apparel oft proclaims the man."

Polonius did not mean that Laertes should be extravagant in the matter of clothes. Far from it; he simply meant that he should dress in a manner befitting his rank as a representative of the court of Denmark.

The salesman is the representative of his

A Salesman's Clothes 147

firm, and to a great extent both he and his firm will be judged by his general appearance, including his clothes,

"For the apparel oft proclaims the man."

CHAPTER XXI

FINDING CUSTOMERS

"Where there's a will, there's a way."
The King is the man who can.—CARLYLE.

THE hardest problem with any business man is to find customers, that is to say, desirable and profitable customers. Identical with the problem of finding customers, is the more difficult one of finding the men who can find the right kind of customers.

There's the rub—"To find *the man who can swim.*" The right kind of salesman will solve for himself this problem of getting customers as he will most others connected with selling. How, you ask? This is how the question was answered recently by a little, short, unprepossessing salesman who is said to have written the largest amount of life insurance in one of the largest insurance companies in the world.

Some time ago this salesman went to Canada

Finding Customers 149

and at an influential gathering saw a man whom he sized up as a good prospect. He got his name and address, found out all about him, his habits and hobbies, one of which was the success of a big hospital in which he was especially interested. Next day the salesman went to this hospital, and asked to be shown through it, after which he called on his prospective customer, told him he had heard of his interest in —— Hospital, and said, "I have been studying this hospital, also; it is doing splendid work, and I would like to make a little contribution to its funds." He thereupon wrote out a check for $250.00 and handed it to this man. *This check was the entering wedge for a $250,000.00 life insurance policy,* which this resourceful salesman soon after wrote for the man whose pet hobby was the big hospital in question.

The main trouble with most salesmen is that they put the problem of finding customers up to the sales manager or heads of the company. They want them to do all the thinking in the matter of where to go, and how to proceed in this difficult business. Let me say right at the start; there is no iron-clad rule for finding customers. Some say it is just a matter of "plan

150 SELLING THINGS

and push," as illustrated in the above instance.

The Sheldon Course in Salesmanship gives five ways for finding a customer, namely; Advertising, Window Display, General or Door to Door Canvass, Selected List Canvass, and Following Up "Leads" or Inquiries.

Many books have been written on the various forms and values of advertising. It is a well-known fact that much money is wasted through injudicious advertising, but no successful business man can dispense with the right kind of publicity. Whether he uses the newspapers, or the magazines, bill-boards, or cards in street-cars, or novelties, will all depend on the goods and the various conditions which have to be met in the marketing of his particular product. Different kinds of advertising should be adapted to each particular territory.

A salesman quickly becomes familiar with such conditions as affect different places and different seasons, so that he plans his campaigns accordingly. Where a man has a fixed territory and is handling goods which are used by a restricted class of people, then the matter becomes relatively simple, although it is important to be always alert, so as not to miss any

FINDING CUSTOMERS 151

possible customers, and so as to learn well in advance about new firms who may want your goods.

A specialty salesman will have to use more originality in finding customers than would have to be used, ordinarily, in the wholesale or retail business, where the home office, or the head of the firm, can map out pretty well just what people should be reached, and how to reach them. Many salesmen lose a lot of valuable time, and waste much money chasing from one town to another, or from one part of a city to another, following up so-called "leads." Unfortunately, the majority of these "leads" are answers to advertisements which were so alluring, and seemed to promise so much for nothing, that a large number of curiosity seekers have written to the home office, with little thought of buying, and more often with little ability to buy, what was advertised.

The salesman who has the courage "*to go to it,*" without any "lead" or point of contact, is the one who will ultimately make the biggest success.

If you have something to sell, do not be afraid to walk into a man's place of business

152 SELLING THINGS

and introduce yourself, telling just what service you are prepared to render. The only good reason for being in business is because you can render service. You should feel that you are the benefactor of the man whom you approach. He may be your superior financially, but in the matter of your particular article or articles for sale, you should feel that you are his superior, and therefore you should approach him with the utmost ease and confidence. The big winners in salesmanship are those who possess the initiative, the originality, and the poise, which enable them to go out and find customers quickly and intelligently, covering the biggest amount of territory in the shortest time, and concentrating their energies.

The use of the telephone in finding customers and making appointments is a method that requires considerable skill. There are those who believe that it is too easy for a man to "turn you down" on the telephone. There are others who believe that it is foolish to waste carfare and time, when you can quickly arrange matters over the telephone. Experience and native ability must guide the salesman in the use of the telephone.

FINDING CUSTOMERS 153

So, in the matter of letter-writing,—often where a letter would be thrown in the waste-basket, or receive a negative reply, a personal call from the salesman might get a big order. Yet, in many cases the right kind of letters would get the business and save the salesman much useless expenditure of time, money and energy.

The day may come when, if our goods are exactly as represented, customers will make a beaten track to our door, but this will not happen until human nature has changed very much. The human element enters so much into sales that it is still quite an important part of salesmanship for the salesman to make personal visits, so as to get the orders. To be sure, we have the department stores and specialty houses which have built up a well-known reputation for merchandise of high quality and reasonable price. These will continue to draw customers, with the help of wise advertising, but they must employ the right kind of sales-force to handle properly the customers who visit their places of business.

Finding a customer does not mean simply inducing him to look over what you have to

154 SELLING THINGS

sell. It means actually inducing him to make a purchase, and satisfying him so thoroughly that he will continue to do business with you. It is because finding the customer is so vitally important that the selling end of a business continues to be, by long odds, the most important department.

No better advice can be given, to sum up, than this: If you would find customers, study all the means and ways in your power; keep thinking, thinking, thinking, and the right thoughts will come, then act, act, act. Never wait for to-morrow. "To-morrow" is a loser. It will never find customers.

CHAPTER XXII

WHEN YOU ARE DISCOURAGED

The man who has acquired the power of keeping his mind filled with the thoughts which uplift and encourage, the optimistic thought, the cheerful, hopeful thought, has solved one of the great riddles of life.

"Don't hunt after trouble, but look for success,
You'll find what you look for, don't look for distress;
If you see but your shadow, remember, I pray,
That the sun is still shining, but you're in the way;

"Don't grumble, don't bluster, don't dream and don't shirk,
Don't think of your worries, but think of your work.
The worries will vanish, the work will be done,
No man sees his shadow who faces the sun."

A YOUNG salesman who has mastered himself and also the secret of success recently wrote from the field:

"Yesterday it seemed as though everything was going against me. There appeared to be something the matter everywhere I called, and although I put up a most determined fight failure after failure met me, until very late in the evening. I had not then taken a single

156   SELLING THINGS

order, but I made up my mind that I could not go back to my boarding place until I had done a decent day's work.   It was this resolution that saved the day, for I took fifteen orders before I got home at nine o'clock.   If I had given up to my discouragement I should simply have said to myself, 'What's the use? This day is gone and I might as well go home, take it easy, and make the best of it.'   But I said, 'No, young man, you are not going to bed to-night until you have done a good day's work.'

"Many a time such a resolution has saved me when, otherwise, I would have made a miserable showing.   I just make up my mind that no matter what attractions come in my way, no matter what discouragements I meet, I will conquer before the night or I will stay up all night.   I find that victory usually follows such a resolution."

The prospect feels the influence of such a determination on the part of the salesman. We radiate our moods, our discouragement, or our courage.   The man we approach feels what we feel, and when we approach him with the spirit of a conqueror, when we go to him with victory in our face, we generally win out.

When You Are Discouraged 157

A notably successful salesman says that he made his first great hit after overcoming a fit of deep discouragement, consequent on the loss of his position. When he got another place he said he started out the first morning with one word ringing in his mind, "Determination." He resolved not to return without an order. He was determined to make that day a red letter day in his life, to show his new employer what was in him, to convince his prospects. He approached every one that day with the determination of victory uppermost in his mind.

"One man afterwards told me," he said, "that I overwhelmed him with my dead-in-earnestness, won him by my determination."

The power of the mind, whether favorable or unfavorable, is tremendous. When a man gives way to discouragement he loses his grip and begins to go down. The bottom seems to drop out of things, and everything helps him the way he is going. His thought connects him with all the thought currents of misfortune, poverty and failure. He attracts those things, for it is a psychological law that failure attracts failure, discouragement more discour-

158 SELLING THINGS

agement, poverty more poverty. To a salesman discouragement is fatal, for when a man assumes the discouraged, failure attitude, he loses power and magnetism, there is nothing inspiring in him, and he not only loses confidence in himself but his fellow men also lose confidence in him. You will find it next to impossible to make a sale with a mind filled with discouragement, pessimistic, failure thoughts.

The exercise of a little will power is all that is necessary for the control of our moods, to change discouragement and depression into courage and hope.

We all know how quickly a child will work itself into a fearful spasm simply by beginning to pity itself. The more he indulges in self-pity, the louder and louder will he cry, until he completely upsets his mind and becomes hysterical.

When inclined to be blue and discouraged, men and women are like children. The temptation is to begin to pity ourselves, then we go on hanging up more dark pictures on the walls of the mind, until we have our whole mentality dressed in mourning. It is not very difficult at the beginning of a discouraged mood to shut

When You Are Discouraged 159

it off by resolutely turning our minds in the opposite direction. Instead of adding to our depression by pitying ourselves the thing to do is to tear down the black flags, the hideous pictures, the gloomy visions of our imagination, to clear them all out of the mind, and let in sunlight and joy, peace and happiness. These will very quickly drive away the gloom and discouragement, and they are just as ready to enter our minds and to stay with us as their opposites, if we will only make room for them.

When you feel downhearted and mentally depressed; when, perhaps, business is dull and you begin to fear you won't make any sales this trip, go somewhere where you can be alone and give yourself an audible self-treatment. If this is not possible, then give yourself a silent or mental one, the form in both cases may be the same. But the audible treatment is apt to be more effective, since the spoken word makes a deeper impression than that which is merely thought or passed through the mind.

Say to yourself something like this: "I am a child of God, I have a living, vital connection with the great Sourse and Sustainer of all

160 SELLING THINGS

things which nothing can sever. Therefore I have nothing to fear. I have strength and ability to do whatever it is necessary for me to do. I was made to be successful, to be happy. This is my birthright and nothing can rob me of it. I will succeed in everything I undertake to-day. I will be cheerful and happy. *I am happy,* because I was made for joy and gladness, not for gloom and sadness. They are foreign to my nature, and I will have nothing more to do with them."

Just fill your mind with good, cheerful, uplifting thoughts and you will find that your feeling will quickly correspond with your mental attitude. After a few minutes of this auto-suggestive treatment you will be surprised at the complete transformation of your outlook. It is astonishing how we can brace ourselves up by auto-suggestion, replacing the distressing, blue, discouraging thoughts with cheerful, hopeful, optimistic thoughts.

There are men who are usually quite level-headed but who do the most foolish things when discouraged or suffering from the "blues," acting under the influence of their moods, when the brain is clouded, inexact,

WHEN YOU ARE DISCOURAGED 161

uncertain in its processes, instead of clear, active, and well balanced.

Discouragement colors the judgment.

Whenever you see a person who has been unusually successful in any field, remember that he has usually thought himself into his position; his mental attitude and energy have created it; what he stands for in his community has come from his attitude toward life, toward his fellowmen, toward his vocation, toward himself. Above all else, it is the outcome of his self-faith, of his inward vision of himself; the result of his estimate of his powers and possibilities.

Self-depreciation is one of the characteristics of those suffering from the "blues." Most of us do not encourage ourselves enough by optimistic thinking, by auto-suggestion.

If you are a victim of your moods, push right into the swim of things, and take an active part, as well as a real interest, in what is going on around you. Associate with people. Be glad and happy, and interest yourself in others. Keep your mind off yourself. Get away from yourself by entering with zest into the family plans, or the plans and pleasures of others about you.

SELLING THINGS

The expelling power of a contrary emotion has a wonderful effect upon the mind. The cure for bad moods is to summon good ones to take their places in the thought and thus force them out.

I know of a woman who was prone to fits of of the "blues," who conquered them by forcing herself to sing bright, joyous songs, and to play lively, inspiring airs on the piano whenever she felt an "attack" coming on.

Do not let anybody or anything shake your faith that you can conquer all these enemies of your peace and happiness, and that you inherit an abundance of all that is good.

If we were properly trained in the pyschology of mental chemistry, we could change the state of our mind as quickly as we can change our clothing. The simple fact, however, that *two opposite thoughts or emotions cannot live together an instant* gives us the key to the whole matter. Every sane person can control and guide his mind. He can choose his thoughts, and the good encouraging thought will neutralize the evil, depressing one. It is just a question of holding in the mind the antidote of the thought that is torturing us, robbing us of our birthright, of success and happiness.

CHAPTER XXIII

THE STIMULUS OF REBUFFS

It is defeat that turns bone to flint, and gristle to muscle, and makes men invincible, and formed those heroic natures that are now in ascendancy in the world. Do not, then, be afraid of defeat. You are never so near to victory as when defeated in a good cause.— HENRY WARD BEECHER.

He only is beaten who admits it.

Do not allow yourself to think that you are weak.

The man who has never formed the victory habit is timid, because he does not know that he can conquer; he doesn't know his strength, because he has never tested it sufficiently to know that it will win.

THE manager of a big insurance company not long since asked me what books I would recommend for putting stamina into a salesman who wilted under a direct "No."

"We have in our employ," he wrote, "a fine mannered, well-educated and very intelligent man. We have thoroughly educated him in the technical part of our business and have done our best to perfect him in salesmanship, but he is not attaining the success we believe

SELLING THINGS

he should. His defect is his inability to continue a conversation with a party who abruptly tells him that he is not interested in life insurance. He states that in a number of such instances he has been unable to say a word, his throat becoming dry. From the above description it might appear to you that the man was wanting in courage. We, however, do not believe this to be the case as his record in the past does not justify that conclusion."

How do *you* stand up under a "No"? Do you lose heart? Does your cheerfulness vanish? Are you conquered then and there? Or does it only act as a stimulant to more determined effort? Does it brace you to meet opposition, put you on your mettle, or do you wilt under it?

A salesman who is made of the right stuff thrives upon opposition. He braces up under rebuffs, rises to the occasion in proportion to the difficulties to be overcome.

Socrates said, "If the Almighty should come to me with complete success in His right hand, and an eternal struggle for success in His left, I would take the left." It is through struggle, through bravely meeting and overcoming ob-

The Stimulus of Rebuffs

165

stacles that we find ourselves and develop our strength.

A successful business man tells me that every victory he has gained in a long career has been the result of hard fighting, so that now he is actually afraid of an easily-won success. He feels that there must be something wrong when anything worth while can be obtained without a struggle, Fighting his way to triumph, overcoming obstacles, gives this man pleasure. Difficulties are a tonic to him. He enjoys doing hard things, because it tests his strength, his ability. He does not like doing easy things, because it does not give him the exhilaration, the joy, that is felt after a victorious struggle.

Some natures never come to themselves, never discover their real strength, until they meet with opposition or failure. Their reserve of power lies so deep within them that any ordinary stimulus does not arouse it. But when they are confronted with obstacles, when they are ridiculed, "sat down upon," or when they are abused and insulted, a new force seems to be born in them, and they do things which before would have seemed impossible.

166 SELLING THINGS

Whenever a motive is great enough, an emergency large enough, a responsibility heavy enough, to call out the hidden reserve in our nature, latent energies spring forth which astonish us. The thin-skinned, sensitive salesman succumbs to the first breath of opposition or discouragement.

It is unfortunate to allow the customer ever to say "No," but do not let a "No" overwhelm you. Remember this is your test. If you stick to your guns and don't show the white feather a "No" will bring out the best that is in you. Whenever you hear "No," call to mind men like Napoleon and Grant, who thrived on opposition and rebuffs.

It is not an easy matter to find salesmen who are capable of coping with all sorts of antagonism. But they are the ones in demand. Such men are not easily argued down—they can put up a stiff fight against every kind of opposition. Where the weak salesman retires from the field beaten, the man with grit and stamina is only taking his second breath. He does not let a rebuff or two phase him. Some salesmen are so weak that they cannot even maintain their own individuality in the pres-

The Stimulus of Rebuffs 167

ence of a prospect with a strong, vigorous mentality. He will annihilate their arguments in a twinkle. They fall down before his onslaught and say, "Yes, I guess you're about right, Mr. Blank. I hadn't thought of that before. But I guess you know best." They cannot hold their ground, maintain their arguments, because they allow themselves to be drawn out of their current of mental vibration, to be overcome by the current of the stronger mentality.

I know two salesmen who go out from different houses over similar territory with the same line of goods. One of them sells four or five times as much in a year as the other. One man *starts out with the expectation, the determination to sell,* and, of course, he gets a very large salary on account of his great ability to sell. The other man gets a very small salary, just barely enough to enable him to hold on to his job, because obstacles seem so great to him. He returns oftener with excuses for not selling than with orders. He has not the ability to annihilate difficulties, to overcome obstacles, which the other man has. He brings back to his house small orders, or none, because he can-

168 SELLING THINGS

not overcome the objections of his customers, cannot convince them that they want what he has to sell.

I once saw an advertisement of a big firm for a manager, which, after describing the sort of man wanted, and saying that no other need apply, closed with, *"The man must be able to cope with antagonism."* Now, the trouble with the unsuccessful salesman I speak of is: he is not able to cope with antagonism. He hoists the white flag the moment the enemy confronts him. He has no fight in him, and surrenders before a shot is fired. When a prospect or customer puts up an objection he is done. "Well, I guess perhaps you are right," he says, "it may be better for you not to buy now." This salesman lacks stamina. There is not enough lime in his backbone, not enough iron in his blood. He is a good honest soul, but he lacks the virility that characterizes the great salesman.

Remember that every weak strand in your character, every hindering peculiarity, every unfortunate habit, will cripple your sales and mar your success. Sensitiveness, timidity, shyness, lack of grit or courage, all of these

THE STIMULUS OF REBUFFS   169

weaknesses are virtually cutters-down of your ability to sell. Timid, shy or sensitive people are often morbidly self-conscious. They are always analyzing, dissecting themselves, wondering how they appear, what people think of them. These things keep the mind diverted from its real object and are all destroyers of concentration and power.

Over-sensitiveness is a very serious handicap in salesmanship. The man who is not able to take his medicine with a smile, who is not able to cope with a surly, a cantankerous, a quick-tempered or a sharp-tongued customer, has no place in salesmanship. In other words, a great salesman must be able to carry on his selling campaign at the points where the ordinary salesman falls down. To do this he must not be thin-skinned. He must be able to stand all sorts of abusive talk under which the sensitive, over-refined salesman quails. He must be ready to push on vigorously at the point where the salesman who lacks grit will quit and turn back. He must be able to stand having pepper and salt sprinkled on his sore spots without wincing. He should keep one thing continually in mind: that his business is, at all costs, to make a sale.

170 SELLING THINGS

This does not mean that a good salesman must have a rhinoceros hide; that would make him unfeeling, unsympathetic, and he would lack the human quality which is so essential in salesmanship. Nor does it mean that he should be pugnacious or over-aggressive. It simply means that he must be able to anti-dote and neutralize the prospect's thrusts, however cruel or aggravating. In short, while keeping perfect control of himself, remaining pleasant and agreeable throughout, he must be able to put up a stiff fight, a dignified, manly fight that will leave him master of the situation.

This is where the timid or over-sensitive salesman falls short. He is thrown completely off his base by the vigorous thrusts and arguments of the rough, energetic business man who doesn't stop to choose his words. He feels injured at the slightest reflection upon his ability, his truthfulness, the character of his goods, or his house. I know a salesman of this sort who will never make his mark, who flares up, "gets up on his ear," as they say, whenever his sensitive, sore spots are touched. He lacks that masterfulness and superb confidence in himself which make a salesman proof against

THE STIMULUS OF REBUFFS 171

abuse or opposition. The self-confident man is impervious to the slights or slurs that make the sensitive man shrink into himself. He is too sensible of his own dignity to let them interfere with his business. When the small man, the peppery or morbidly sensitive man, feels that he must protect his "honor," even if he lose a sale, the big, broad man knows that no one can hurt his honor but himself, and that it is best served by refusing to feel hurt or insulted where in reality no insult is intended.

Another point that works to the great disadvantage of the timid or sensitive salesman is this: he is afraid to make what is called the "cold" or "straight" canvass; that is, to approach people without having a "lead" or an introduction. This is a great weakness, and very often false pride is at the bottom of it. The man feels above his task. Again, ignorance of goods or of selling principles will cause a man to lack confidence in himself, and then, naturally, he is timid, fearful, for he foresees the failure that awaits him when he calls on a customer. Ignorance is timid; knowledge is bold, courageous. It is not enough to have possession of yourself if you don't also have

172 SELLING THINGS

possession of your business, that is, if you are not thoroughly grounded in the principles of salesmanship. Thus grounded, if you adopt the right attitude toward your business and toward yourself, nothing can keep you from success.

Throw off your shyness, your morbid sensitiveness, your timidity. Get rid of your lack of faith and courage. Confidently expect that you are going to be a great salesman, a distinctive one, a salesman with individuality, with originality, with inventiveness, a man of resource and power. Never allow yourself to think that anything is true about you that you wish to be otherwise, because the thought you hold in mind is the model of your life building. Think faith, think courage, think strength, and you will develop those qualities.

The reason why so many of us build so slowly and so poorly is because we are constantly destroying our building by shifting our model. One day we have confidence in ourselves, and our mental model is full of courage, hope and expectancy, and the life forces build accordingly. The next day we are in the dumps, have no faith in ourselves, are discour-

The Stimulus of Rebuffs 173

aged, and of course these are the models for that day's building, destroying the building of the previous day, and thus many of us go through life, building up and tearing down.

Be consistently courageous, hopeful, confident in yourself and in the power of your Creator to make you what you long to be, and nobody, nothing on this earth, can down you.

There is everything in flinging out a superb confidence in yourself, a firm belief that you are going to win. Expel all doubt and fear, all uneasiness, from your mind and approach every prospect with the expectation of success.

"Courage," says Emerson, "comes from having done the thing before." Your first success will give you the momentum that will push you on to the next. Every achievement adds to our self-confidence, the great leader of all our other faculties. If confidence does not go ahead, the other faculties refuse to go on.

Every time you conquer what you undertake, you add so much to the power of all the faculties you possess. Just as a snowball grows larger and larger as it rolls down hill, so our lives grow larger, richer, with each experience. We lose nothing of what we achieve. It is all added to the life-ball.

174 SELLING THINGS

Not long ago I asked a very successful man, really a "born salesman," what he considered the essential qualifications for good salesmanship. He put in the first category of qualifications: confidence in your goods, confidence in your firm, and confidence in yourself, plus enthusiasm, plus earnestness, plus perseverance, plus hard work, plus enjoyment of your work. In the second place he put: general knowledge of merchandise. In the third place he put: personality, and under this heading he included, honesty, neatness of appearance, poise, courtesy, sincerity, and temperance. The natural born salesman, he said, possesses all of these things, and in addition, tact, shrewdness, and understanding of human nature.

Now, there is nothing in this list of qualifications that is not within the reach of every honest intelligent youth who has enough stamina and will power to make his life a success.

You are a child of the Infinite; you bear the stamp of the Creator, and you must partake of His qualities. It is up to you, then, to make good; it is your duty as a man to show

The Stimulus of Rebuffs 175

your origin, to stand your ground, to maintain your independence, your self-reliance, your dignity, against all attacks. It is up to you to stand for something in your life work, to be counted as one to be reckoned with in any transaction. It is your own fault if you are sucked out of your own plane of vibrations by a bully, a fighter, by any one, be he great or small. Selling honest goods is an honorable pusuit. Bring out your God-given powers. Improve the qualities He has given you and make your work, make your life significant. Don't be apologetic; don't be afraid; don't cringe or wilt under opposition. Feel the importance and dignity of your work and let others feel that you feel it. Say to yourself, "I too am a son of God, the equal of this or any other man. I am going to maintain my poise, my individuality, my faith in myself, no matter what he says. I am as self-reliant, as independent, as forceful as any other man. I shall not be cowed by any one. I am not going to be downed by an obstacle."

You will find it a wonderful help in overcoming obstacles in every phase of your work to assume a victorious mental attitude, and to

176 SELLING THINGS

carry yourself like a conqueror. If you go about among your fellows with a defeated expression in your face, giving the impression that you are not much of a man anyway, that life has been mostly a defeat, and that you don't look forward to any success worth while, you certainly cannot hope to, and never will, inspire confidence in others; if your face, on the other hand, glows with the expression of victory, if you carry a victorious attitude, if you walk about the earth like a conqueror, a man victory-organized, you are *headed toward victory*. Nothing can keep you from winning out, because—and don't forget this—*Success begins in the mind.*

CHAPTER XXIV

MEETING COMPETITION: "KNOW YOUR GOODS"

"This is the age of push, struggle and fierce competition."

"Study your competitor—his manner and method of doing things."

THERE are certain lines of business in which the salesman has no competition; this, however, is the exception. There are many lines in which the competition is more imaginary than real; that is to say, the quality of the goods of the so-called competitor is so much inferior to that of the goods carried by a first-rate house that there is no real competition. The buyer, however, who is usually shrewd, and, unfortunately, is often unscrupulous, will, if possible, lead the salesman to think that competitors have given better prices or better terms, and that their goods are superior. The salesman who is not armed at every point to meet his tactics runs the risk of being imposed on.

One superlatively good rule is this:—

178 SELLING THINGS

"Know Your Goods." That will enable you to meet both real and imaginary competition. By this we mean, be familiar with the intrinsic merits of the goods you are selling, and know the market conditions which surround the trade. Read very carefully all the literature and advertisements put out by your house. Nothing will destroy a buyer's confidence more quickly than to find a salesman ignorant of the claims made by his own house, or of the specific qualities of the goods offered for sale. Salesmen need to keep themselves fresh and enthusiastic in regard to their goods, not only by thorough reading of their house organs, and all literature issued with the view of creating patronage, but also by getting information from every possible source that will help them in their special line. Outside of what a man can learn from the printed matter furnished by his own house, he may learn much additional from leading trade journals and by talking with men who are familiar, in a practical way, with his line. In getting information from the salesmen of a competing house it is best not to exchange confidences. Learn all you can in an open, fair way, but do not resort to trickery, or

MEETING COMPETITION 179

to any methods which you would be unwilling to have a competitor use with your house.

The second rule for meeting competition is "Know Competitors' Goods." This again involves not only being familiar with the quality and uses of the goods, but with the reputation of the manufacturer and his selling agents, as well as the class of trade to which competitors cater, the class of salesmen they employ, and the ethics they observe in doing business.

Some believe that three-quarters of all business is done on a friendship basis. But it is a different friendship than that meant by the accepted term. It is business friendship, not social friendship.

Naturally, if you do business amicably with a man for a long time you are "friendly." You call each other Smith and Brown, possibly "Charlie" and "Eddie"; maybe you lunch together occasionally. But such friendship is in nowise like that bestowed on your old neighbors, your college classmates, or your club brothers.

Many a man who has started out to do business on a real friendship basis has found out to his sorrow that it can't be done.

180 SELLING THINGS

"Friendship and business don't mix" is an old adage and a true one. You can't presume on your intimacy with a man to sell him goods; and it is seldom you can get his trade away from a successful salesman, even if you have identical goods and quote the same price. The salesman has become the buyer's friend too, in a different way to what you are, but still a friend and deserving of consideration. No doubt business friendship plays a very large part in business getting with all salesmen. You know how hard it often is, to break in on the trade of another man, simply because he has won the friendship of his customers. Keep this in mind, and do everything to win the friendship and merit the continued confidence of your trade.

In this connection, remember that "knocking" is bad. When giving the rule, *"Don't knock,"* as a good one for every salesman, I mean simply that a salesman should not criticise unfairly or bitterly the goods of another. There is no harm in pointing out the real defects or inferiority of rival merchandise, but it is a great mistake to show ill-will or to make unkind, uncalled-for criticisms. If it is neces-

MEETING COMPETITION 181

sary to protect a man from buying what is going to cause him a loss, we should not hesitate in criticizing and pointing out defects, but our criticisms should be made in a tactful way, so as not to leave the impression that we are "soreheads."

In the next place, avoid the great mistake of young salesmen, and of many experienced men, who talk their competitors' goods far too much. I know a salesman of very pleasing personality who frequently hurts his sales in this way. He has a way of scattering his customer's attention by introducing the possibilities of rival products in his own line. At the present time he is selling automobiles, and is constantly comparing his car with others, diverting the customer's attention, by enlarging on the advantages and disadvantages, the good and bad points, of rival cars, confusing a man by bringing into his mind so many things at the same time.

He seems to take delight in exhibiting his thorough knowledge of the points of those other cars, and, in doing so, he often raises a question in the customer's mind as to the desirability of some other than the one the sales-

182 SELLING THINGS

man is selling, and will in many instances postpone purchasing until he investigates the rival cars.

The best salesmen say very little about a competitor's goods. They simply explain and emphasize the advantages and good points of their own.

Don't ignore questions about competitors, and don't fail to banish from the customer's mind all doubts and prejudices, but it is a serious mistake to spend a lot of time talking about competitors' goods, when you ought to be sticking to the merits of your own. Answer quickly all questions, and then switch back to the excellence of what you are selling. Be so enthusiastic about your own selling points that rivalry will be forgotten.

In meeting competition, do not be fooled by the question of price. At present, very many staple lines are of about the same quality and the same price, so that you must bring out, as a high-grade salesman should, the fact that *service is the main consideration*. Show what your house can do in the matter of prompt deliveries, careful packing, dependability as regards uniform quality, correct count, liberal terms,

MEETING COMPETITION

etc., and do not forget that the general reputation of your house is a selling point. The facilities which you have for keeping abreast of the times, like the employing of experts to do experimental work, thereby improving your product all the time, is a point of service well worth consideration.

Not the least important of the methods to meet competition is for the salesman to analyze both the conditions of the people on whom he calls and the territory in which he works, Any suggestions that he may make to his house will help in the matter of educational advertising, which always can be used to advantage in selling.

Above all, a salesman can meet competition most effectively by a strong personality. Remember that your goods are judged by yourself, sometimes, even, unfairly; and remember that we are always judged by our weakest points; hence, in order to hold your old trade from competitors, and to get new trade, you must possess "business magnetism," which is another way of saying "a strong personality."

CHAPTER XXV

THE SALESMAN AND THE SALES MANAGER

Every salesman should feel that he is a partner in the business.

The man who thinks he knows it all is taking a header for oblivion.

IT is of the utmost importance that every salesman should have full confidence in his sales manager. There are many peculiar conditions which exist in all lines of business. The conditions of the trade are best known to those who have reached the position of sales manager or general manager, and their advice should always be sought with an open and receptive mind.

In many lines of business, treating and entertaining play an important part. Often, business can be procured through taking your customer to the theater, or taking him to your club for lunch or dinner, and quite often an afternoon playing golf may be the best way to

SALESMAN AND SALES MANAGER 185

"land" a large contract. There is far less entertaining done nowadays, however, than formerly. Entertaining is always so agreeable for the entertainer, as well as for the customer, that many salesmen are likely to overdo in this respect. They attach too much importance to social meetings outside of the actual getting of orders; hence, it is wise to abide by what the head of the firm, or the sales manager, may think in the matter of just how far to go when expending money, even for cigars that are to be given with the view, not of bribing the customer, but of getting him in a friendly attitude of mind.

Always be open-minded at the weekly or daily meetings, when instructions are given by the sales manager. Do not refer to his words as "hot air" and "bunk." If you have suggestions, do not hesitate to call his attention to what you think would be helpful to the other men. Remember that if you really *know* more than the sales manager does, it is not going to be long before you will have *his* job. If you only *think you know* more than he does, and you persist in showing this, either by words or actions, you will soon lose *your* job.

186 SELLING THINGS

Written instructions from a sales manager are the best kind. He would always do well to sum up briefly the main points of his advice, and get them out in the form of a letter or bulletin. Half a page of typewritten ideas, containing a few words of inspiration, will work wonders, both for the discouraged and for the enthusiastic members of his force.

To get the best results, sales managers should always be friendly and sympathetic with their men. Harsh criticisms upset a man, sometimes, to the extent that he will be worried and nervous for several days. Positive and emphatic reprimands are often called for, but they should always be courteous and tactful.

And the salesman, when listening to the criticisms of his sales manager, should remember this old quotation, "Better the wounds of a friend than the kisses of an enemy."

Sales managers of the old school believe that finding fault and harsh, driving methods will get the best results. They are mistaken. "You can get more flies with molasses, than you can with vinegar," is a saying perfectly true in its application alike to the salesman and the sales manager. This does not mean that the

SALESMAN AND SALES MANAGER 187

weak-kneed, spineless manager can get good results. Being friendly does not mean losing dignity. Different men must receive different treatment. There are lazy men, untidy men, those who do not try to make the most of whatever ability they have, and men with other more or less grave faults. In dealing with these, it is necessary to "lay down the law" much more emphatically than with the timid but ambitious ones.

Marshall Field was in the habit of saying to his employees, "Remember that the customer is always right." I would advise every salesman to keep in mind these words: "Remember, your sales manager is always right."

A matter you must invariably refer to your sales manager is that of swaying your customer by gifts. Many people want something for nothing, and a salesman often thinks that the easiest way to get an order is to use one or another kind of bribery. This may take the form of rebates, or cash on the spot, or presents. Be very discreet in such matters.

As a scientific salesman, do not forget to consider the buyer. He is buying scientifically. He is suspicious. Every one is trying to drive

188 SELLING THINGS

a very close bargain. He tries to make you yield on price, to make some concessions on payments, to give special privileges about returning goods, etc. Beware of all these tactics. Here, again, you must consult frequently, and with confidence, your sales manager. He knows the tricks of your particular trade, and he will be able to give you proper coaching.

Be sure, above all things, that if your sales manager had a chance to put an epitaph on your tombstone it would not be this: "He meant well, tried a little, and failed much."

CHAPTER XXVI

ARE YOU A GOOD MIXER?

Charm of personality is a divine gift that sways the strongest characters, and sometimes even controls the destinies of nations.

The art of the salesman is akin to that of the orator. Both seek the mastery of the mind, the sympathy of the soul, the compulsion of the heart.

Personal magnetism in a man corresponds to charm in a woman.

An attractive, pleasing personality makes a striking first impression.

"Getting what you want from kings or statesmen," De Blowitz said, "is all a matter of dining with the right people." Through the power of his charming presence, his gracious manner, this famous journalist accomplished greater things at the dinner table, in the drawing-room or ball-room than any other newspaper man in Europe accomplished through letters of introduction, influence and special "pulls." His popularity, his power to interest and please others, was his strongest asset.

190 SELLING THINGS

The ability of Charles M. Schwab to make friends, his strong social qualities, his faculty for entertaining, for making himself agreeable, played a powerful part in his rapid advancement from a dollar-a-day job to the position of millionaire steel manufacturer. It was his social qualities which first drew Mr. Carnegie so strongly to him.

During the Homestead troubles, according to reports, young Schwab used to cheer Mr. Carnegie with humorous stories and the singing of Scottish ballads, and the iron master was always in better spirits after a visit from the young man.

There is no other one thing in such universal demand everywhere, in social life and in business, as the power to attract and please. A magnetic personality often commands a much bigger salary than great ability with a disagreeable personality.

I have in mind a young business man, with such a captivating manner, with such power to interest and please, that there are many firms in this country which would pay him a fabulous salary for his services.

We all like to do business with people who

ARE YOU A GOOD MIXER? 191

attract us. If we could analyze cracker-jack salesmen in this country, we should find that they are men who have a fine magnetic personality. They are great "mixers," they understand human nature. They are usually men of broad sympathies, are large-hearted, and of magnanimous natures.

"Diamond Jim" Brady—James Buchanan, he was christened,—is a shining example of the ultimate salesman. Mr. Brady has advanced himself to the position of selling rolling stock and supplies to railroads, and occasionally he sells entire railroads, making enormous fees as broker. He is perhaps the personification of "personality" and as a "mixer" he has no peer. His name is synonymous with "good fellow," and his list of acquaintances is said to be as large as that of any other one man in New York.

There is something about one's personality which eludes the photographer, which the painter cannot reproduce, which the sculptor cannot chisel. This subtle something which every one feels, but which no one can describe, which no biographer ever put down in a book, has a great deal to do with one's success in life.

192 SELLING THINGS

It is this indescribable quality, which some persons have in a remarkable degree, which sets an audience wild at the mention of the name of a Lincoln or a Blaine,—which makes people applaud beyond the bounds of enthusiasm. It was this peculiar atmosphere which made Clay the idol of his constituents. Although, perhaps, Calhoun was a greater man, he never aroused any such enthusiasm as "the mill-boy of the slashes." Webster and Sumner were great men, but they did not arouse a tithe of the spontaneous enthusiasm evoked by men like Blaine and Clay.

A historian says that in measuring Kossuth's influence over the masses, "we must first reckon with the orator's physical bulk, and then carry the measuring line above his atmosphere." If we had discernment fine enough and tests delicate enough, we could not only measure the personal atmosphere of individuals, but could make more accurate estimates concerning the future possibilities of schoolmates and young friends. We are often misled as to the position they are going to occupy from the fact that we are apt to take account merely of their ability, and do not reckon this personal atmosphere

Are You a Good Mixer? 193

or magnetic power as a part of their success capital. Yet this individual atmosphere has quite as much to do with one's advancement as brain-power or education. Indeed, we constantly see men of mediocre ability, but with fine personal presence, being·rapidly advanced over the heads of those who are infinitely their superiors in mental endowments.

Walt Whitman used to say that a man is not all included between his hat and his boots. This is but another way of putting the fact, proved by science, that our personality extends beyond our bodies. It is not who we are, how we are dressed, or how we look, whether we are homely or handsome, educated or uneducated, so much as what we are that creates that subtle mysterious atmosphere of personality which either draws people to us or drives them from us.

If you are exclusive; if you always want to keep by yourself and read, even though it be for self-improvement; if you love to get in a seat by yourself when you travel; if you shrink from mixing or getting acquainted with others on the road or in hotel lobbies; if people bore or irritate instead of interest you, you will never

194 SELLING THINGS

make a great salesman. You must be a good mixer, a "good fellow" in the highest sense of the word (not a dissipater) ; you must be popular because of your lovable human qualities, or you will not have that peculiar drawing power which invites confidence and attracts business. No matter what other excellent qualities he may possess, the exclusive man is rarely, if ever, magnetic; he doesn't draw people to him; on the contrary, he keeps them at a distance.

I know of an exclusive salesman of this sort who for lack of this drawing quality is making a very poor showing in his business. Although a splendid fellow in many respects, a man of high ideals and sterling honesty, he is not popular, because he has never learned to be a mixer, never learned to be a good fellow, to approach people with a smile and a cheery greeting, to hold out the glad hand of fellowship.

When he registers in a hotel, even if he has been there many times, he just bows to the clerk, secures his room, and retires to it at once. He loves books, is quite a student, but he does not care to be with people any more

Are You a Good Mixer? 195

than he can help. The other traveling salesmen do not like him. His distant, dignified personality repels them. In a word, his exclusiveness and his lack of magnetism have largely strangled his effectiveness as a salesman.

It takes warm human qualities to make a good salesman. You cannot sell things by the use of mere cold technique, however perfect. You must establish sympathetic, wireless connection with the prospect's mind by making him feel that you are not only very much of a man to start with, but that you have a lot of human sympathy, and are really anxious to serve him, to put a good thing in his way.

Some salesmen have no more real sympathy for their prospect than they would have for a Hindoo image. Their voices carry no more sympathy, no more real human feeling than a talking machine. The house that employs them might as well send out phonographs to repeat their mechanical salesman story. They may hold customers who know that the firm they represent has an excellent reputation, but they have no power to attract new ones.

There is no other factor which enters so

196 SELLING THINGS

largely into success in business, in social, and in professional life, as does personality. There is nothing else which has such an influence in our dealings with others.

It is one of the salesman's greatest assets. It will make all the difference in the world to him whether he is sociable, magnetic, with an attractive, agreeable, cheerful temperament, or whether he is grouchy, cranky, disagreeable and arouses antagonism in those with whom he deals.

It is not always the man of the greatest ability, the greatest mental power, by any means, who makes the great salesman. A man may be a mental giant; he may have a Websterian brain and yet be a pigmy of a salesman. A pleasing, attractive personality is a tremendous drawing power.

It has the same advantage a sweet, beautiful girl has when you first meet her. The girl doesn't have to try to make a good impression; her personality, her charm, her grace do this without any effort on her part. I have heard merchants say they looked forward with keen pleasure to the coming of a certain salesman because he was such a good fellow; he was so sociable, cheery and agreeable.

Are You a Good Mixer? 197

It is a very difficult thing to resist that magnetic charm of personality which has swayed judges and juries from justice, and has even changed the destinies of nations. We have not the heart to deny or refuse, to say "No" to the man or woman who grips us with the impalpable force of a magnetic personality.

When logic and argument fail, when genius says "impossible," when pluck and persistency give up, when influence has done its best and quits, when all the mental qualities have tried in vain, the subtle something which we call personal magnetism steps in and without apparent effort wins.

It makes a tremendous difference whether you bring a personality to your prospect which makes a striking, pleasing first impression, or whether you bring a cold, clammy, unenthusiastic, unresponsive nature, which makes an indifferent or an unfavorable impression, one that you must endeavor to overcome with a lot of long, tedious arguments. It is the personal element which makes the chief difference between the great salesman with a big salary and the little fellow with a little salary. The little fellow may try just as hard as the big fellow,

198 SELLING THINGS

indeed he may try much harder; he may have had a better training in the technique of salesmanship, but because he lacks the warm, sympathetic, human, sociable qualities, his industry and hard work are largely neutralized.

I know a man who through the force of his personality is a colossal power in attracting business. Men follow him, are attracted to him, just as needles are attracted to a magnet. They can't very well help dealing with him, he gets such a magnetic grip upon them. He does not need to make a very strong appeal; his personality speaks for him.

Phillips Brooks had such a personality. Strangers who passed him on the street felt his power to such a degree that they would turn and look after him. In his presence none could resist the pull of his magnetism, of his most wonderful personality. I was once a member of his Sunday School class in Trinity Church, Boston, and every one in the class instinctively felt from the first that he was in the presence of a great, a superb specimen of humanity. He had such tremendous magnetic power that when he wanted money for any charitable or philanthropic purpose, he did not

Are You a Good Mixer? 199

have to beg for it, he merely suggested the need of it, and the closest pocketbooks would fly open. Everybody believed in Phillips Brooks because of the power of his superb character, the magnetism of his remarkable personality.

Emerson says, "What you are speaks so loudly that I cannot hear what you say." We cannot conceal what we are, how we feel, because we radiate our atmosphere, our personality; and this is cold or warm, attractive or repellent, according to our dominant traits and qualities.

A person who is selfish, always thinking of himself and looking out for his own advantage, who is cold, unsympathetic, greedy, cannot radiate a warm, mellow atmosphere because one's atmosphere is a composite and takes on the flavor of all of one's qualities. If selfishness, indifference, avarice and greed are dominant in one's nature, this is the kind of an atmosphere he will radiate and it will repel because these qualities we instinctively detest.

The qualities that attract are out-flowing, buoyant; the qualities that repel are in-flowing; that is, people who have no magnetism are self-centered, they think too much about them-

200 SELLING THINGS

selves; they do not give out enough; they are always after something, absorbing, receiving some benefit, trying to get some advantage for themselves. They lack sympathy, lack cordiality, good fellowship; they are bad mixers.

Some people are naturally magnetic, but when you analyze their character you will find they possess certain qualities which we all instinctively admire, the qualities which attract every human being, such as generosity, magnanimity, cordiality, broad sympathies, large views of life, helpfulness, optimism.

There is not one of these qualities that the salesman can not cultivate and strengthen a great deal. If he does so he will get a hearing where others have thrown back at them the fatal words, "No time to see you to-day—very busy."

Many upright, honorable young men with political aspirations have been thwarted in their election campaign because they did not know how to make themselves popular. Splendid young men, striving for political honors, are constantly being beaten by men much their inferior in many respects. And this not because of graft or pull on their opponents' side, but

ARE YOU A GOOD MIXER? 201

because the latter are good mixers. They know how to meet people, how to be good fellows, how to mix with others; in short they know how to make themselves popular.

We all know what a great demand there is in every line of business for traveling salesmen who are good mixers, men who have a genius for interesting, attracting and holding customers.

Whatever your business, your reputation and your success will depend in a great degree upon the quality of the impression you make upon others. It means everything, therefore, to young men, and to young women also, to develop a magnetic, forceful personality.

This is not a very difficult thing to do. Every one can cultivate the ability to please and the strength of character that will make him felt as a real force in the world. Knowing the qualities and characteristics that distinguish the magnetic and the unmagnetic, it is comparatively easy for us to cultivate the one and to eliminate the other. That is, we can cultivate the generous, magnanimous, cheerful, helpful mental qualities and crush their opposites; and in proportion as we do this

202 SELLING THINGS

we shall find ourselves becoming more interested in others, and they in turn becoming more interested in us. We shall find ourselves more welcome wherever we go, more sought after; we shall attract people to us more and more, as we make ourselves personal magnets by fashioning our aura of the kindly thoughts and words and deeds that day by day go to the making of a rich, magnetic personality.

In other words, if you cultivate the qualities which you admire so much in others, the very qualities which attract you, you will become attractive to others. Just in proportion as you become imbued with these qualities so that they shall characterize you, will you acquire a magnetic, attractive personality.

A good education is a great advantage to a man or a woman, but most of us put too great emphasis upon education, upon mental equipment and training. We seem to think that this is everything, but our personal atmosphere may have more to do with our success in life, more to do with determining our place in the world, our social or business advancement, our standing in our community, than our mere mental equipment.

Are You a Good Mixer? 203

The first step toward making yourself magnetic is to build up your health. Vigorous health, coupled with a right mental attitude, an optimistic, hopeful, cheerful, happy mind, will increase your magnetism wonderfully.

A person having robust health radiates an atmosphere of strength, a suggestion of vigor and courage, while one who lacks vitality drains from others instead of giving to them. Physical force and abounding joyousness of health help to create a magnetic, forceful personality. The man with buoyant, alert mind, with a sparkle in his eye and elasticity in his step, the man who is bubbling over with abundant physical vitality, has a tremendous advantage over those who are devitalized and are weak physically.

To be magnetic you must face life in the right way. Pessimism, selfishness, a sour disposition, lack of sympathy and enthusiasm— all of these tend to destroy personal magnetism. It is a hopeful, optimistic, sunny, sane, large-hearted person who radiates the kind of personal magnetism we all admire, the kind that commands attention, that attracts and holds all sorts of people.

204 SELLING THINGS

Above all if you want to have a magnetic, attractive personality, cultivate the heart qualities. Intellect, brain power, has little, if anything to do with personal magnetism. It is the lovable, not the intellectual, qualities that draw and hold people. You must make people feel your sympathy, feel that they have met a real man or a real woman. Don't greet people with a stiff, conventional, "How do you do?" or "Glad to meet you," without any feeling, any sentiment in it. Be a good mixer and adapt yourself to different dispositions. Look every person you meet squarely in the eye and make him feel your personality. Give him a glad hand, with a smile and a kind word which will make him remember that he has come in contact with a real force, which will make him glad to meet you again.

If you would be popular, you must cultivate cordiality. You must fling the door of your heart wide open, and not, as many do, just leave it ajar a little, as much as to say to people you meet, "You may peep in a bit, but you cannot come in until I know whether you will be a desirable acquaintance." A great many people are stingy of their cordiality. They

ARE YOU A GOOD MIXER? 205

seem to reserve it for some special occasion or for intimate friends. They think it is too precious to give out to everybody.

Do not be afraid to open your heart; fling the door of it wide open. Get rid of all reserve; do not meet a person as though you were afraid of making a mistake and doing what you would be glad to recall.

You will be surprised to see what this warm, glad handshake and cordial greeting will do in creating a bond of good-will between you and the person you meet. He will say to himself, "Well, there is really an interesting personality. I want to know more about this lady or gentleman. This is an unusual greeting. This person sees something in me, evidently, which most people do not see."

Some people give you a shudder, and you feel cold chills creep over you when they take hold of your hand. There is no warmth in their grasp, no generosity, no friendliness, no real interest in you. It is all a cold-blooded proceeding, and you can imagine you hear one of these chilling individuals say to himself, "Well, what is there in this person for me? Can he send me clients, patients or customers?

206 SELLING THINGS

If he does not possess money, has he influence or a pull with influential people? Can he help or interest me in any way? If not, I can not afford to bother with him."

Cultivate the habit of being cordial, of meeting people with a warm, sincere greeting, with an open heart; it will do wonders for you. You will find that the stiffness, diffidence and indifference, the cold lack of interest in everybody which now so troubles you will disappear. People will see that you really take an interest in them, that you really want to know, please and interest them. *The practice of cordiality will revolutionize your social power.* You will develop attractive qualities which you never before dreamed you possessed.

If you cultivate a magnetic personality you will increase your sales and lessen your work, besides getting a lot more enjoyment out of life than you otherwise would.

Remember, customers are drawn, not pushed. Trade to-day is largely a question of attraction, and the salesman who is the most magnetic, who has the most affable manners, who is a good mixer, will attract the largest amount of orders.

CHAPTER XXVII

CHARACTER IS CAPITAL

Character is greater than any career.

Manhood overtops all titles.

CHARACTER is the greatest power in the world. Nothing can take its place; talents cannot, genius cannot, education cannot, training cannot. The reputation of being absolutely square and clean and straight, of being a man whose word is his bond, is the finest recommendation.

Simple genuineness, transparency of character, will win the confidence of a customer whether he is prejudiced or not, and the confidence of the purchaser is half the sale, for no matter how pleasing the speech or the manner of the salesman, if he isn't genuine, if he doesn't ring true, if he doesn't inspire confidence, if the customer sees a muddy streak back of his eye, he is not likely to purchase.

Lack of absolute integrity often keeps sales-

208 SELLING THINGS

men in inferior positions. Take the average salesman in a retail clothing store. A customer tries on a coat. "How does it look?" he asks the salesman in a pleased tone.

"Perfect, fine," answers that worthy.

Then a garment of totally different cut is put on. If the customer seems to like it, the salesman echoes his view. It is just the coat he should buy.

Pretty soon the customer realizes that the salesman's advice is worthless; he won't tell him the truth as to how the garment looks, fits and hangs; he is intent only on making a sale. When the customer sees this, naturally he will not buy there. He will go to another house or to a salesman who will tell him the truth, who will be honest with him.

Sincerity, genuineness, transparency, carry great weight with us all. Just think what it means to have everybody believe in you, to have everybody that has ever had any dealings with you feel that, there is a man as clean as a hound's tooth and as straight as a die; no wavering, no shuffling, no sneaking, no apologizing, no streak of any kind in his honesty; you can always rely on his word. There is a young

CHARACTER IS CAPITAL 209

man who has nothing to cover up; he has no motive but to tell the truth; he doesn't have to cover up his tracks because he has lied once and must make his future conduct correspond; he knows that honesty needs no defense, no explanation. His character is transparent. One doesn't need to throw up guards against him.

We all know what a comfort it is to do business with such a man, a man who cannot be bought, who would feel insulted at the mere suggestion that any influence could swerve him a hair's breadth from the right. Is there anything grander than the man who stands four-square to the world, who does not love money or influence as he loves his reputation, and who would rather be right than be President?

The salesman who has made such a reputation, a reputation of never misrepresenting, never deceiving, never trying to cajole or over-influence, who never tries to sell a man what he knows he does not want or what would not be good for him, who does not try to palm off "out of season" goods or cover up defects, is certainly a comfort and a treasure both to his employer and his customers.

210 SELLING THINGS

How much more comfortable and satisfactory it is for oneself not to have to watch every step and to guard every statement for fear one will let out some previous deception! How much easier and how much better it is to be honest than always to have to be on the lookout for discrepancies in one's statements, to be obliged continually to cover one's tracks!

No training, no bluffing, no tricks, will take the place of genuine sterling character; your prospect's instinct, if he is a sharp student of human nature,—and most business men are,—will very quickly tell him whether you are shamming an interest in him or whether it is genuine. He can tell whether you are pure gold or a base counterfeit; and if your character is unalloyed you will establish a friendly relation with him which will be of very great value.

A good salesman will not fail to realize that the men he approaches have been swindled many times, and that a hooked trout is shy of new bait. He will not forget that his would-be customers probably have had many unfortunate experiences, that possibly they have bought many gold bricks, that their confidence

CHARACTER IS CAPITAL 211

has been shaken many times by violated pledges, so that they will be on their guard, and at the outset will look upon every salesman who approaches them as a smooth-tongued swindler. The experienced man knows that business chickens come home to roost, that a dishonest policy, any underhand business, any effort to take advantage will surely be a boomerang for the firm. It is only a question of time. Every misrepresentation, every mean transaction will sooner or later cost the firm very dear.

Remember that every sale you make is an advertisement that will either help or hinder your business. It is an advertisement of the character and general policy of your firm. It advertises the squareness, the honesty, or the cunning, the trickery of the whole concern; in other words, the man you approach will get a pretty good idea of your firm,—their policy and methods of doing business,—by the impression which you make on him. He can tell pretty well whether he is dealing with high-class men, whether he can absolutely depend upon the word of the house, whether he can rely upon their statements, whether he will be

212 SELLING THINGS

protected, or whether he will have to protect himself by watching and guarding every little step in every business transaction with the house. He can tell whether he can rely absolutely upon its doing the square thing by him or not. "A company is judged by the men it keeps."

The best salesmen to-day, besides making a study of their business, make a study of their customers and their wants. Many customers regard such salesmen as their business advisers, and they give them their confidence, knowing they will receive from them "white" treatment, that they will only sell them the merchandise which it is to their advantage to buy.

After he has gained their confidence it would be easy enough for the salesman to violate it and sell a much larger bill of goods than is to the advantage of the customer, but the modern salesman knows that this is a poor sort of business policy. The old-time method of holding up a customer when you get him for every dollar you can squeeze out of him, and piling onto him just as many goods as he can be induced to take, and at the biggest possible price, has gone by forever.

CHAPTER XXVIII

THE PRICE OF MASTERSHIP

"Three things are necessary, first, backbone; second, backbone; third, backbone."—CHARLES SUMNER.

"When other people are ready to give up we are just getting our second wind," is the motto of a New York business house. A good one for the success aspirant.

> "Ships sail west and ships sail east,
> By the very same winds that blow;
> It is the set of the sails, and not the gales,
> That determines where they go."

"WRECKS of the world are of two kinds," said Elbert Hubbard. "Those who have nothing that society wants, and those who do not know how to get their goods into the front window."

The way to succeed in salesmanship is to get your goods into the front window and hustle for all you are worth. Hard work and grit open the door to the Success firm.

Two college students started out to sell copies of the same book. After some weeks in the field one wrote to headquarters as an ex-

213

214 SELLING THINGS

cuse for his poor business that "everything had been trying to keep him down of late." The weather had been so bad he could not get out a great deal of the time; then everybody was talking "hard times," and no money, and making all sorts of excuses for not buying. He said he was so disgusted and discouraged that he saw nothing for it but to give up canvassing as a bad job.

The other young man, canvassing in similar territory, sent in his report about the same time. This is what he wrote: "In spite of bad weather and the fact that everybody is trying to hedge on account of the war scare and the general business depression I have had a banner week, and my commissions were over eighty dollars. I get used to this 'hard times and no money,' and 'can't afford it' talk, and I just sail right in and overwhelm all these objections with my arguments. I make the people I talk to feel that it would be almost wicked to let the opportunity pass for securing a book, the reading of which has doubled and trebled the efficiency of a multitude of men and women and has been the turning point in hundreds of careers. I have made them feel that it

THE PRICE OF MASTERSHIP 215

will be cheap at almost any price, and that I am doing them a great favor in making it possible for them to secure this ambition-arousing book."

This young man sold, on the average, to eight people out of ten he called upon during the week.

A traveling salesman for a big concern got it into his head that his territory out through the West was played out. His orders were shrinking, and he told his employers that the territory had simply been worked to a finish, that there was no use in staying in it any longer. His sales manager, however, knew the section well, and doubted the man's glib statement. He put a young fellow in his place who had had very little experience, but who was a born hustler, full of energy, ambition and enthusiasm. On his first trip he more than doubled his predecessor's record. He said he saw nothing to indicate a played-out route, and was confident that business would increase as he became better acquainted with the territory.

The fact was that, not the territory, but the man was played out. The older salesman was

216 SELLING THINGS

not willing to forego his comforts, his pleasures, to hustle for business. He was not willing to travel across the country in bad weather on the chance of getting an order in a small town. He preferred to remain in the Pullman cars, to go to the larger towns and sit around in hotel lobbys, to take things easy, to go to the theaters instead of hunting up new customers and making friends for the house. He wanted his "dead" territory changed, because he had no taste for hustling. His successor did not see any lack of life in that "played-out" route because he was "a live wire." The trouble was not in the territory; it was in the man.

At an agricultural convention while discussing the slope of land which was best suited to a certain kind of fruit tree, an old farmer was called upon to express his opinion. He got up and said, *"the slope of the land don't make so much difference as the slope of the man."* It isn't the slope of the territory that counts so much in selling as the slope of the salesman; that is everything. In every business it is always a question of the sort of a man behind the proposition. It is the slope of

THE PRICE OF MASTERSHIP   217

the man, his grit, his stick-to-it-iveness, that count most.

No matter how letter perfect you may be in the technique of salesmanship, or how well posted on all the rules of effective procedure, if you lack certain qualities you never will make a first-class salesman.

If you lack grit, industry, application, perseverance; if you lack determination and that bulldog grip which never lets go or knows when it is beaten; if you lack sand, you will peter out. Having these qualities you will overcome many handicaps.

I have known a little sawed-off dwarf of a salesman to wade into a prospect and, through sheer grit, get an order where the ordinary salesman, with good physical appearance, would have failed.

This fellow said that grit had been his only capital in life; that when he found he was so handicapped by his size and his ugly features that he would probably be a failure and a nobody in the world, he just made up his mind he would not only overcome every one of his handicaps, but that he would be a big success in his line. He did everything he had resolved

218 SELLING THINGS

to do, and through sheer force of grit "made good." He had paid the price of success, and won out, as will every one who is willing to pay the price.

Only the weakling prates about "luck," a "pull," or "favoritism," or any other backstairs to success. Your success and your luck are determined by yourself and by no other. We are the masters of our destiny. We get just what *we want*. To be sure, all of us *wish* for a lot of things; we would like very much to have them, but we don't really want them, or we would straightway set to work and try very hard by every means in our power to get them. Many of us wish for a position worth anywhere from ten thousand dollars to one hundred thousand dollars a year, but we want to get it without much effort, and to hold it with still less effort. What we really want is success without effort, an easy job at the highest market price, like the cook pictured in a recent cartoon, applying for a place. Her first question is: "And what's the wages, mum?" "Oh, I always pay whatever a person's worth," answers the employer. " No, thank ye, mum. I never works for as little as that," replies the disgusted would-be employee.

The Price of Mastership 219

Let us remember that there is no easiest way to success in any business or profession. We are here to develop ourselves to the highest point of our ability; to be the broadest, ablest, most helpful men and women we can be, and this is only possible through the assiduous cultivation of our highest faculties. We can only grow and progress through self-development. No patent method has yet been discovered by which a man or woman can be developed from the outside.

Abraham Lincoln tells us, "The way for a young man to rise, is to improve himself every way he can, never suspecting that any one wishes to hinder him."

Hudson Maxim, the famous inventor, has formulated ten success rules, the essence of which are, study and work. He makes two vital assertions: 1. "Never look for something for nothing; make up your mind to earn everything, and remember that opportunity is the only thing that any one can donate you without demoralizing you and doing you an injury." 2. "Man must eliminate from his mind any belief that the world owes him a living."

220 SELLING THINGS

Now, some people differ with Mr. Maxim on this last point. They believe the world does owe each one of us a living. If they are right, it is pleasant to think that the world is very ready to pay this debt, when we come around to collect it in the right way. If we can do any one thing superbly, no matter how humble it may be, we shall find ourselves in demand. The world will most willingly pay its indebtedness to us.

Men and women who have won distinction in every business and profession are unanimous in their agreement as to two cardinal points in the achievement of success—Work and Grit.

The Honorable Thomas Pryor Gore, the blind Senator of Oklahoma, who raised himself from a poor, blind boy to be an influential member of the United States Senate, has this to say on the secret of pushing to the front: "A fixed and unalterable purpose, pursued under all circumstances, in season and out of season, with no shadow of turning, is the best motive power a man can have. I have sat in physical darkness for twenty-seven years, and if I have learned anything it is that *the dyna-*

The Price of Mastership   221

mics of the human will can overcome any difficulty."

Here, indeed, is encouragement for every youth in this land of opportunity. Think of a poor, blind boy, unaided, achieving such distinction as Mr. Gore has won! Think of a blind Milton writing the greatest epic in the world's literature! Think of a Beethoven, stone deaf, overcoming the greatest handicap a composer could have, and raising himself to the distinction of being one of the greatest composers the world has known! One of this wonderful man's sayings is well worth keeping in mind by every young man struggling with difficulties: "I will grapple with fate; it shall never drag me down."

It is well also to remember this truth: "Usually the work that is required to develop talent is ten times that necessary for ordinary commonplace success." Men naturally brainy, or with some great gift, have to work most assiduously to achieve big results. Without untiring perseverance, industry, grit, the courage to get up and press on after repeated failures, the historic achievers of the world would never have won out in their undertakings.

222 SELLING THINGS

Columbus said that it was holding on three days more that discovered the New World; that is, it was holding on three days after even the stoutest hearts would have turned back that brought him in sight of land.

Tenacity of purpose is characteristic of all men who have accomplished great things. They may lack other desirable traits, may have all sorts of peculiarities, weaknesses, but the quality of persistence, clear grit, is never absent from the man who does things. Drudgery cannot disgust him, labor cannot weary him, hardships cannot discourage him. He will persist no matter what comes or goes, because persistence is part of his nature.

More young men have achieved success in life with grit as capital, than with money capital to start with. The whole history of achievement shows that grit has overcome the direst poverty; it has been more than a match for lifelong invalidism.

After all, what do all the other accomplishments and personal decorations amount to if a man lacks the driving wheel, grit, which moves the human machine. A man has got to have this projectile force or he will never get very

THE PRICE OF MASTERSHIP 223

far in the world. Grit is a quality which stays by a man when every other quality retreats and gives up.

For the gritless every defeat is a Waterloo, but there is no Waterloo for the man who has clear grit, for the man who persists, who never knows when he is beaten. Those who are bound to win never think of defeat as final. They get up after each failure with new resolution, more determination than ever to go on until they win.

Have you ever seen a man who had no give-up in him, who could never let go his grip whatever happened, who, every time he failed, would come up with greater determination than ever to push ahead? Have you ever seen a man who did not know the meaning of the word failure, who, like Grant, never knew when he was beaten, who cut the words "can't," and "impossible," from his vocabulary, the man whom no obstacles could down, no difficulty phase, who was not disheartened by any misfortune, any calamity? If you have, you have seen a real man, a conqueror, a king among men.

As we look around at other men, enjoying

SELLING THINGS

the good things of life, basking in the sunshine of success, let us remember that they didn't get their place in the sun by wishing and longing for it. They didn't get to Easy Street by the road of Inertia. When you are tempted to envy those people, and long to have a "pull" or some one to give you a "boost," just call to mind this jingle:

"You must jump in, and fight and work, nor care for one defeat;
For if you take things easy, you won't reach Easy Street.
Don't waste time in envy, and never say you're 'beat,'
For if you take things easy, you won't reach Easy Street."

There is no royal road to anything that is worth having. Only work and grit will do the trick. As J. Pierpont Morgan says, "Hard, honest, intelligent work will land any young man at the top."

The great business world is always on the hunt for the man who can do things a little better than they have been done before, the man who can deliver the goods, the man who can manage a little better, the man who is a little shrewder, a little more scientific, a little more accurate, a little more thorough; it is always after the man who can bring a little better brain, a little better training to his job.

The Price of Mastership 225

With our constantly widening national interests, our enormously expanding trade, the demand for A1 salesmen is ever on the increase. The young man who is not satisfied with the ordinary required equipments for salesmanship, but who will add to this a thorough knowledge of modern languages, especially those most used in commercial intercourse—German, French and Spanish—will not have very great difficulty in finding his place in the sun.

The making—or the marring—of your life is in your own hands. "The gods sell anything and to everybody at a fair price." Success is on sale in the world market place. All who are willing to pay the price can buy it. In the final analysis, success in salesmanship, as in everything else, is simply a matter of "paying the price."

CHAPTER XXIX

KEEPING FIT AND SALESMANSHIP

To keep fit is to maintain perfect health; and perfect health depends upon a perfect balance of mind and body, unimpaired physical vigor and absolute inner harmony, a mental poise which nothing can disturb.

There is a vast amount of ability lost to the world through poor health, through not keeping in condition to give out the best that is infolded in us.

"I WANT you," said Philip D. Armour to one of his employees, "to grow into a man so strong and big that you will force me to see that you are out of place among the little fellows."

If you want to be a salesman "so strong and big" that you will be "out of place among the little fellows," you must be as physically fit as was John L. Sullivan in his prime. At that time the mere sight of Sullivan entering the ring struck such terror into the heart of his opponent that the fight was half won before a blow was struck. It seemed to the small

KEEPING FIT AND SALESMANSHIP 227

man like a desperate venture to tackle a giant with such a superb physical presence. The famous pugilist's appearance had as much to do with his success as had his knowledge of the technique of the ring.

If you want to win out (and who does not?) you must enter the ring—the arena of life— with all the power you can muster, in superb health, at the top of your condition, capable of putting up your biggest fight. You can do this and come out with your flag flying if you are good to yourself, if you keep fit. But if you allow all sorts of leaks of power to drain away your energy, your brain force, your will power, you will be in no condition to make the fight of your life.

You should be as well prepared physically for the contest as the prize fighter who is determined to keep his record. Or, like the Greek god Hercules, you should be able to win largely by the force of your reserve power. It was said that Hercules made such an impression of great reserve force on his antagonist that he never had to put forth much strength in wrestling. He won as much by the impression of confident power which he

228 SELLING THINGS

radiated, as by the degree of strength he exerted.

In other words, if you do not back up your general ability and special training with robust health you will be forever at a disadvantage in the game of life. You must keep yourself fit for your job, always in a condition to do your best or you will be handicapped in the game.

It is the law of life that the "weakest shall go to the wall." Frailness of body is an inevitable handicap in life. Physical weakness largely discounts the possibilities of achievement. The slow but striving tortoise may beat out the hare in the race. The steadfast, plodding student may take the prizes of life which his more brilliant competitor never attained. But the tortoise, though slow, is sound of body. Cripple him and all his plodding will avail him little.

True, there have been weak men who have done wonders in life in spite of frailness and physical infirmity. But they are only the exceptions that prove the rule. Alexander Pope, "the gallant cripple of Twickenham," sewed up in canvas; St. Paul, short in stature,

KEEPING FIT AND SALESMANSHIP   229

of inferior presence and almost blind, are types of the men whose great souls overcame their bodily weakness. Cæsar, Pascal, Nelson, were other types of the indomitable spirit which can not be limited by sickness or infirmity. But, in the main, the man who "makes good" has good health.

As a salesman you carry all your capital with you. You are in business, but you carry everything connected with it, your factory, your sales department with you. Your machinery assets are mental, and if you don't do your best to keep them in fine condition you will show about as much sense as a farmer who would leave all his valuable farm machinery out-doors in all sorts of weather, to be ruined by wind and dew, rain and snow. Your skill, your expertness, your facility of expression, your tact, your discretion, your power of discrimination, your knowledge of human nature, your courage, your initiative, your resourcefulness, your cheerfulness, your magnetism, in fact, every one of your mental faculties is a part of your business capital, is an asset, and its condition depends entirely on the care you take of the engine which furnishes

230 SELLING THINGS

the motor power for all your mental machinery. That engine is your body.

The physical soil is the soil in which your faculties are nourished. If this soil is impoverished, if your vitality is low, if you are sapping your energies by vicious, ignorant, or foolish habits, your faculties will not thrive.

Some time ago an ambitious young fellow came to me and asked me to tell him how to increase his ability and his power to achieve things. He was pale and emaciated, with something like signs of dissipation in his face. The young man seemed very anxious to get along in the world but, evidently, he had taken the wrong path. A few questions brought out the fact that although not dissipating in the ordinary sense, the course he was pursuing was almost as disastrous to his health. He was sitting up till one or two o'clock at night, studying, while working very hard in the daytime, and to brace up his depleted strength he was not only drinking coffee and tea to excess, but he was also taking whiskey, and even drugs. He did not seem to know that this artificial stimulus to his brain was like a whip to a tired horse, and that it was only a question of

Keeping Fit and Salesmanship 231

time until he would be a physical and mental wreck.

It is amazing how ignorant many otherwise intelligent people are when it comes to a question of body and health building. Young people often ask me to tell them how they can increase their ability, and in nine cases out of ten I find that, like the young man above, they are doing some fool things that defeat the very object they have in view.

Now, the surest way to increase your ability, to multiply and strengthen your faculties, is to lay a good foundation of health, and to guard it as you would your most precious possession—for that is really what it is. Vigorous, abounding health will emphasize, reinforce and multiply the forcefulness of all the faculties, and the sum of these faculties constitutes your ability, the force that achieves, that creates.

It will make a tremendous difference to you what sort of a man you take to your prospect. I say "you take," because you are the master of the salesman. There is something bigger back of the salesman, than the salesman himself. You are the salesman's manager, his

232 SELLING THINGS

trainer, his educator. There is a master in you, who, to a very large extent, dictates the sort of a man "you take" to your prospect, because he will be the sort of a man *you* make him. To be a whole man, mentally, physically, and spiritually is your business. To be deficient on any of these planes is to be only two parts a man. To be one hundred per cent. a man—that is your problem.

The human machine is very complicated, and even a little thing may seriously impair its harmony and efficiency. A bad fitting shoe may cut down your effectiveness temporarily, or as long as you wear it, twenty-five per cent. A speck of dirt in the eye would cripple a Napoleon, as a hair in the works would seriously injure the best timepiece in the world. A hasty, bolted lunch, of poor, adulterated food, may impair your digestion, cut down your brain power and make you ineffective when it is of the utmost importance that you be effective.

Efficiency lies in the symmetry and perfect functioning of all of your organs. If they are not trying to help you make a sale; if you have treated them badly and they are protest-

KEEPING FIT AND SALESMANSHIP 233

ing, they will beat you. You may think that, no matter how you feel, you can put a deal over by sheer will power, but remember that your will power is dependent upon the harmonious action of all your bodily functions. It will weaken just as soon as any one of these is impaired. If not one, but several of them—your digestive organs, your liver, your heart, your kidneys, your brain, are fighting against you, trying to defeat your purpose, you will not win out no matter how hard a fight you put up. Many a superb salesman has finally lost out by making an enemy of all the organs which make for health and success.

Do you realize what goes into every sale you make? Did it ever occur to you that your brains, your education, your training, your experience, your skill, your ingenuity, your resourcefulness, your originality, your personality—about all your life capital is flung into every selling transaction?

The result of every canvass you make will depend very largely upon how much of yourself you fling into it, and how intensely, how enthusiastically, cheerfully, and tactfully you fling yourself in. You cannot bring the whole

234 SELLING THINGS

of yourself to the sale unless every function of your body gives its consent. Your physical organism must be in perfect harmony or your vitality will be lowered, and you will be robbed of a certain percentage of your possible power.

The great thing when you approach a prospect is to be all there, not to leave ten, fifteen, twenty or twenty-five per cent. of yourself in the bar-room or in some other vicious resort the night before. Do not fling a lot of your ability away in bad food, or in a too rich and complicated diet, viciously taken. Be sure when you call on a prospect that you take a good digestion along with you; it is the best friend of your brain. If your digestion is ruined by over-eating, or if your brain is not well fed, no amount of will power, or cocktail or whiskey braces, will compensate for the loss you suffer.

Many a promising salesman has failed to make good because he made a habit of turning night into day and could take only about half of himself to his work. Many a cracker-jack salesman has lost a sale by partaking too heartily of dinner, or by a fit of indigestion brought on by some indiscretion in eating.

Multitudes of people go through life work-

KEEPING FIT AND SALESMANSHIP 235

ing hard, trying desperately to succeed, but are terribly disappointed by the meagerness of their achievement, simply because they did not take care of their health. They are all the time devitalized; they lack blood, or it is of poor quality; it lacks fire and force, and, of course, the brain and all the faculties deteriorate to correspond with the blood.

The achievement follows the vitality, and this in turn depends on the general care of the body. The kind of food, its quality and amount, the manner in which we partake of it, our physical habits, work, rest, recreation, sleep,—these are the things on which health and vitality depend. These furnish our physical energy and achievement depends upon energy. It would be impossible even for the brain of a Webster to focus with power, if fed with poor ill-nourished blood.

Everywhere we see bright, educated young men and women, with good brains, crippled by poor health, mocked by great ambitions which they can never realize. A large part of their ability is lost to the world because of some physical weakness which might be remedied by careful, scientific living.

236 SELLING THINGS

Just glance over the young men you know and see what a small part of their ability goes into their life work, because of their impaired assets, through foolish or vicious living habits. They are selling their integrity, squandering their life capital in all sorts of dissipation, bringing perhaps not more than twenty-five per cent. of their actual ability to their life work.

How often we hear the remark: "Poor fellow! he was always a victim of bad health, but for that he would have accomplished great things." "Mentally able but physically weak" would make a good epitaph for thousands of failures.

A weakness anywhere in you will mar your career. It will rise up as a ghost all through your life work, at unexpected moments, mortifying, condemning, convicting you. Every indiscretion or vicious indulgence simply opens a leak which drains off your success and happiness possibilities. There is no compensation for waste of health capital. Health raises the power of every faculty and every possibility of the man, and there is no excuse for losing it through carelessness, dissipation or ignorance.

Keeping Fit and Salesmanship 237

Nor can one plead mere weakness or lack of energy as a handicap, an excuse for failure. Nature is no sentimentalist. If you violate her law you must pay the penalty though you sit on a throne. She demands that you be at the top of your condition, always at your best, and will accept no excuse or apology.

Whatever your work in life, the secret of your success and happiness is locked up in your health, in your brain, your nerves, your muscles, your ambition, your ideal, your resolution. It is up to you to be a whole man. You cannot afford to be less. You cannot afford to dwarf your career or botch it by going to your task with stale brains. You cannot do first-class work with second-class brain power, with a brain that is fed by poison,—blood vitiated by abnormal living or dissipation. You cannot afford to go to your work used up, played out. Trying to sell merchandise with stale brains keeps many a salesman capable of real mastership in a mediocre position. You cannot do a master's work with a muddy brain which was not renewed, refreshed, by plenty of sound sleep, healthful

238 SELLING THINGS

recreation, and vigorous exercise in the open air.

In other words, if you expect to make the most of yourself you must be good to yourself. Strangled health means strangled ability. If you murder your health you murder all your chances in life.

No man ever does a great thing in this world who does not protect the faculties he is using with jealous care. Watch your generating power. Remember that you see the world largely through your stomach. Its condition will determine the condition of your brain. Poor digestion gives you poor blood, and poor blood a poor brain. Few people realize what a tremendous factor health plays in their success. Men give the brain credit for a large amount of their success which is due to the stomach, which has everything to do with physical health and robust vitality.

Not long ago I was talking to a salesman who said he guessed he was losing his grip; didn't know how it was, but he was not making sales as he used to. He didn't have the same grit and enthusiasm; guessed he was sliding down hill, going backward instead of forward.

KEEPING FIT AND SALESMANSHIP 239

Formerly, he said, he always approached a customer with the expectation of getting an order, but latterly he was in great doubt; he could not get on full steam, a resolute determination to win. Now, when a man gets into this condition he is not fit to solicit business. Nature is calling to him: "Stop, Look, Listen." It is time for him to call a halt, and see what is the trouble with his engine.

If you would be a master in your specialty heed Nature's danger signals, which she puts up all through your body. That "tired feeling" is one of them; brain fag, headache, is one of them; indigestion is one of them; apathy, "don't feel like it," poor appetite,—all these things are signals to slow down. But instead of slowing down and repairing, most of us try to speed up with all sorts of stimulants and run past these danger signals, with the result that we either wreck our life train or very seriously injure it.

No man can afford to ignore Nature's warnings, but least of all can the salesman, on whose physical condition everything depends. Other men can depute their work, at least for a time, to those under them; but the salesman cannot

240 SELLING THINGS

do this, for he is strictly a one-man concern, and everything depends on his health. He must always be at the top of his condition; and every quality needed in his work is sharpened and braced by vigorous health.

How comparatively easy it is, for instance, for a healthy man to be hopeful, optimistic, enthusiastic. How difficult for a chronic dyspeptic to be any of these—to be kind, gentle, generous, cheerful, obliging. His natural disposition may not be at fault, for the tendency of ill health is to make a man cross, crabbed, fault-finding, fretful, hard, pessimistic.

"Touchiness," a defect which makes so many men and women unbearable, usually comes from some weakness or physical ailment. A great many so-called "sins" are due to a depleted physical condition. It is so much easier for a man to control himself when he is well, to say "No" with emphasis, when, if he were suffering from some physical disability, he might say "Yes,"—anything to get rid of annoyance and to get into a more comfortable condition.

How much health has to do with one's manners! How easy to be courteous and accommodating when one feels the thrill of health

KEEPING FIT AND SALESMANSHIP 241

surging through his whole being; but how hard to be polite, gentle, amiable, when one feels ill, weak, and nervous, and wants to be let alone! How hard to carry on an interesting conversation when all of one's physical standards are down!

Then again, how the health affects the judgment! The judgment is really a combination of a great many other faculties, and the condition of each seriously affects the quality of the combination.

One's courage is largely a matter of physical health. How quickly the ailing man, to whom everything looks blue, becomes discouraged! Everything looks black to people whose physical standards are demoralized.

Horse trainers know that a horse's courage during the contest depends a great deal upon its being in a superb physical condition. It is the same with the horse's master—man. Courage, poise, masterfulness, resourcefulness, physical vigor go together. Nervousness, timidity, uncertainty, doubt, hesitation, usually accompany depleted vitality.

The bull-dog tenacity which plays such a part in every life worth while has a physical

242 SELLING THINGS

basis. The will power, which is a leader in the mental kingdom, depends very largely upon the health. How different, for example, obstacles look to the man who is ailing all the time, suffering pain, compared with the way they look to a man who is full of vigor and energy. The man who is well plans great things to-day, because he feels strong and vigorous. Obstacles are nothing to him; he feels within himself the power to annihilate them. But to-morrow he is ill, and the obstacles which were only molehills yesterday, loom up like mountains, and he does not see how he can possibly conquer them.

We look at things through our moods, and moods are largely a question of physical health. The man who is strong and full of the courage of abounding vitality wants something hard to wrestle with; he feels the need of vigorous exercise. But the man whose vitality is low has no surplus to spare. Slight difficulties look formidable to him; trifles are exaggerated into serious obstacles, which seem insurmountable. There is confusion all through his mental kingdom, and his faculties will not work harmoniously. There is a tremendous wear

KEEPING FIT AND SALESMANSHIP 243

and tear on the physical economy of the man in poor health.

The faculty of humor was given man to ease him over the jolts, to oil the bearings of life's machinery; but ill health often crushes out the sense of humor, and makes life, which was intended to be bright and cheerful, sad and gloomy. Loss of good red blood corpuscles has much to do with one's sense of humor as well as one's manners and disposition. The man in poor health is in no condition to appreciate the joys of life. Everything loses its flavor in proportion to his lowered vitality.

Ill health very materially weakens the power of decision. A man who, when in vigorous health, decides quickly, finally and firmly, when in poor health, wobbles, wavers, reconsiders. His purpose, which was once a mighty force in his life, lacks virility, has lost much of its strength. In fact, all of his life standards drop in proportion to the decline in physical vigor.

Again, the quality of health has a great deal to do with the quality of thought. You cannot get healthy thinking from diseased brain cells or nerve cells. If the vitality is below par the thought will drop to its level.

244 SELLING THINGS

What magic a trip to Europe or a vacation in the country often produces in the quality of one's thought and work. The writer, the clergyman, the orator, the statesman, who was disgusted with what his brain produced comes back to his work after a vacation and finds himself a new man. He can not only do infinitely more work with greater ease, but his work has a finer quality. The writer is often surprised at his grip upon his subject and his power to see things which he could not get hold of before. There is a freshness about his style which he could not before squeeze from his jaded brain. The singer who broke down comes back from a vacation with a power of voice which she did not even know she possessed. The business man returns with a firmer grip upon his business, a new faculty for improving methods, and a brighter outlook on the world. The brain ash has been blown off the brain cells which were clogged before; the blood is pure; the pulse bounding, and, of course, the brain cells throw off a finer quality of thought, keener, sharper, more penetrating, more gripping.

Many a salesman could add twenty-five or

KEEPING FIT AND SALESMANSHIP 245

fifty per cent. to his power by easing the strain of life now and then, especially when Nature hangs out any of her warning signals.

Supposing an Edison or some other great inventor should discover a secret for doubling one's ability, what would we not all do or give to get this secret? Yet every one knows a process for doubling ability which never fails. It is health-building, vitality-building, by simply exercising common sense in the matter of living. There is nothing complicated in this; it means eating just enough, not too much or too little, of the foods that give force and power, scientific eating of these foods; scientific care of ourselves, exercise, recreation, play; getting out of doors whenever possible and absorbing power from the sun and air; getting plenty of sleep in a well-ventilated bedroom; regular systematic habits; right thinking, triumphant thinking, holding the victorious attitude toward life, toward our work, toward our health, toward everything. Now here is the secret of doubling ability. We all have it; all that is necessary is to put it in practice.

There is no other thing that will pay a salesman better than putting it in practice every

246 SELLING THINGS

day. Keeping himself in superb physical condition will not only give a wonderful flavor to life, but it will add great interest and charm to his personality. Good health is the foundation of personal magnetism; it is the secret of the sparkle in the eye, the buoyant spirit, the keen whip to the intellect which sharpens all the wits. Many a sale has been clinched by the pleasing appearance of a salesman, the charm of a bright, flashing eye, a clear skin, a firm step, and a straight pair of shoulders.

How quickly we can tell by the appearance of horses on the street what sort of care they get. How fine a carefully groomed horse looks and how well he feels. He seems to have a sense of pride in his personal appearance, whereas the horse which is seldom if ever groomed, shows his neglect by the sharp contrast.

The same thing is true of individuals. I have a friend who takes infinite pains to keep himself in prime condition. He says his human machine is his most precious asset and that he cannot afford to neglect his exercise; he cannot afford to be irregular in his eating habits, or to eat foods which are not body builders,

KEEPING FIT AND SALESMANSHIP 247

health and force producers; he cannot afford to lose sleep, or to do anything which will lower his vitality. He is equally careful about his grooming, and always looks fit, in the pink of condition. Another friend of mine is just the opposite. He will take a hot bath in about ten minutes; he dresses in a hurry; never bothers about his exercise or his food, and the result is the two men present as great a contrast as the well-groomed, well-cared for horse and the ill-groomed, ill-cared for one.

It is of little use to have all the qualities which make a good salesman if these qualities are not kept in prime condition. Yet there are a great many salesmen who do not take time enough to care for themselves properly, to keep their wonderful machine in fine trim, in superb physical and mental condition.

It was said that Ole Bull could never be induced to go on playing unless his violin was in perfect tune. If a string stretched the least bit, no matter how many thousands were waiting for him, he would stop until he had put his violin in perfect tune again. Ole Bull would not allow himself even for a moment to be anything but a master.

248 SELLING THINGS

You cannot go to your prospect with the brain of a master salesman, victory-organized, if your instrument is out of tune. If you do not keep yourself tuned to concert pitch; if you do not take the trouble to make a fine adjustment of your wonderful human instrument each day; if you do not put yourself in tune each morning for the day's work; if there is the least inharmony in any of the marvelous mechanism of your body, you will go on all day producing discord instead of harmony. In other words, you will be a failure instead of a success.

When you approach a prospect be sure you are "in tune with the Infinite," (with the highest law of your being) that you are all there, that you are not sixty, seventy-five, eighty, ninety or ninety-nine per cent. present, but that you are all there, that you are a hundred per cent. present, and that this hundred per cent. is ready to strike the blow. More will depend upon your body and mind being in complete harmony, in perfect tune than on all of your special training in salesmanship.

In this age of fierce competition physical vigor plays a tremendous part. It is an age

KEEPING FIT AND SALESMANSHIP 249

of efficiency force, an age which requires masterfulness. The victors in the great life game to-day, as a rule, are men with powerful vitality, tremendous staying power. Whether you win out or lose in the game will depend largely on your reserve power, your plus vitality.

Keep yourself always fit so that you can do your best, *the highest thing possible to you,* with ease and dignity, without struggle or strain, and you will be a master salesman. Always be at the top of your condition, and you can approach your prospect with the assurance of victory, the air of a conqueror, with the superb confidence that wins. Keep your human machine in perfect tune, and you will radiate power, masterfulness; you will exhale force and magnetism from every pore; you will be the sort of salesman that every customer is glad to see—A MASTER SALESMAN.

APPENDIX

SALES POINTERS

"THERE are two chief classes of men that you will approach.

"One class is ruled chiefly by reason, the other by impulses—emotion—prejudices—enthusiasm—likes and dislikes.

" The first class can be convinced only by hard matter-of-fact, mathematical arguments —the kind of evidence that will pass a judge in court. The minds of these men are clear, cold, logic engines. They are impressed only by facts and figures, and will do no business with salesmen who offer them anything else.

"The other class—of impulsive or emotional men—is amenable to heart sway persuasion.

"You will not find it so necessary to convince their reasons. Give them the best evidence you have, but mix it with something more.

"Be careful of their prejudices, watch out for the revelation of their likes and dislikes,

SALES POINTERS

251

discover their enthusiasm, suit yourself to their moods.

"Sooner or later, if you know your business, you will uncover the vulnerable spot in an emotional man and he is yours. Strike him with the right kind of persuasion and you can walk out with his order.

"Study your prospects. Learn to read the book of human nature. The formulas for success in selling are written on its pages."

✻ ✻ ✻

Don't be a slave of precedent. It is an enemy of progress. Know the technique of salesmanship, but don't be its slave. Study men at the top and then ask yourself, "Why can't I do what they have done? RESOLVE NOT TO BE A LITTLE FELLOW.

✻ ✻ ✻

No matter how much you know about salesmanship your personality, your character, will be the chief factors in your success.

While the technique of salesmanship is important, yet it is the man behind the salesman that does the business. It is the human power back of the mere technique that makes the sale.

252 Selling Things

THREE KINDS OF SALESMEN

The Heavyweight,
The Featherweight, and
Just plain WAIT. —Selected.

✢ ✢ ✢

"Some salesmen are not always successful salesmen—BUT, successful salesmen are always SOME salesmen."

✢ ✢ ✢

"A master salesman is a self-made salesman —BUT a self-made salesman isn't always a master salesman."

✢ ✢ ✢

Always keep in mind the man at the other end of the bargain. If he does not make a good bargain you will lose in the end, no matter how much you may sell him.

✢ ✢ ✢

Follow your prospect's mind. Let him do much of the talking. If he sees you are trying to push him and expecting to change his mind he will brace up against you.

✢ ✢ ✢

THE SALESMAN'S CREED

To be a man whose word carries weight at my home office, to be a booster, not a knocker,

SALES POINTERS 253

a pusher, not a kicker; a motor, not a clog.

To believe in my proposition heart and soul; to carry an air of optimism into the presence of possible customers; to dispel ill temper with cheerfulness, kill doubts with strong convictions and reduce active friction with an agreeable personality.

To make a study of my business or line; to know my profession in every detail from the ground up; to mix brains with my effort and use method and system in my work. To find time to do everything needful by never letting time find me doing nothing. To hoard days as a miser hoards dollars; to make every hour bring me dividends in commissions, increased knowledge or healthful recreation.

To keep my future unmortgaged with debt; to save money as well as earn it; to cut out expensive amusements until I can afford them; to steer clear of dissipation and guard my health of body and peace of mind as my most precious stock in trade.

Finally, to take a good grip on the joy of life; to play the game like a gentleman; to fight against nothing so hard as my own weakness and to endeavor to grow as a salesman and

254 SELLING THINGS

as a man with the passage of every day of time. THIS IS MY CREED.—W. C. HOLMAN.

✢ ✢ ✢

Salesmanship is the ability to sell the largest possible quantity of goods, to sell an increasing quantity of goods, to get the greatest possible results from the advertising done by his house, to make a regular customer of a new buyer, and to hold the friendship of a regular customer.—H. E. BOWMAN.

✢ ✢ ✢

Never sit down or stand, if you can possibly avoid it, below where your prospect is seated. The man who is the highest always has the advantage, the superior position. Many salesmen can do better standing while the prospect is sitting.

✢ ✢ ✢

Approach your prospect as a professional, not as an amateur, not as a little fellow, or *almost* a salesman, but approach him with the air of a professional. Give him to understand that you are no third-rate salesman. Your manner will have everything to do with the impression you make.

SALES POINTERS 255

Establish confidence as quickly as possible. Business men are constantly dealing with mean, tricky men, unscrupulous men, hypnotizers, bull-dozers, but when they strike the real article, the genuine man, they will give him their confidence.

✤ ✤ ✤

Remember your whole success will often turn on the first two or three minutes of your interview. Just here your knowledge of human nature is a tremendous factor. You must size up your man quickly and find the line of least resistance, the best approach to his mind. Not only his temperament but his health, the frame of mind he happens to be in, all must be taken in at a glance.

✤ ✤ ✤

Be a tactful salesman. You will often be told that tact cannot be cultivated, that it is a quality that is born in one, but remember that every man is tactful when he is courting the girl he is dead in love with. If you are dead in love with your work and bound to win you will be tactful.

✤ ✤ ✤

256 SELLING THINGS

Make it an invariable rule never to use any influence or to say anything in the presence of a prospect which will lessen your self-respect. If you do, you lose power. *You are not paid for being less than a man.*

✤ ✤ ✤

A real salesman sells goods. Fakers sell customers. Don't be a mere order-taker; be a salesman.

✤ ✤ ✤

ANOTHER "SALESMAN'S CREED"

"I believe in the goods I am handling, in the company I am working for, and in my ability to get results.

"I believe that honest stuff can be passed out to honest men, by honest methods.

"I believe in working, not weeping; in boosting, not knocking, and in the pleasure of my job.

"I believe that a man gets what he goes after; that one deed done to-day is worth two deeds to-morrow, and that no man is down and out until he has lost faith in himself.

"I believe in to-day and the work I am doing; in to-morrow and the work I hope to do,

SALES POINTERS 257

and in the sure reward which the future holds.

"I believe in courtesy, in kindness, in generosity, in good cheer, in friendship, and in honest competition.

"I believe there is something doing somewhere for every man ready to do it.

"I believe I am ready right now."

✢ ✢ ✢

Do you ever go to see a prospect expecting to be turned down—to meet unanswerable arguments or deep-rooted prejudices that you can't overcome? If you do, it's pretty likely that that's what happens.

✢ ✢ ✢

Half-knowledge is worse than ignorance.

MACAULAY.

✢ ✢ ✢

This is one business man's motto: "Nothing pays like quality." There is a whole sermon in this motto, for what is there that pays like quality? There is no advertisement like it. Quality needs no advertisement, for it has been tried. Talk quality. A high-class salesman tries to convert his prospect from a lower to a higher grade, for there is not only greater

258 SELLING THINGS

satisfaction but also larger profit both for seller and buyer in the high grade article.

✻ ✻ ✻

Did you ever realize that when you are working for another you are really selling yourself to him, that your ability, your education, your personality, your influence, your atmosphere—everything about you is sold for a price? Every time you sell goods you are selling part of yourself, your character, your reputation, what you stand for—it is all included in the sale.

✻ ✻ ✻

Progress depends upon what we are, rather than upon what we may encounter. One man is stopped by a sapling lying across the road; another, passing that way picks up the hindrance and converts it into a help in crossing the brook just ahead.—TRUMBULL.

✻ ✻ ✻

Fate does not fling her great prizes to the idle, the indifferent, but to the determined, the enthusiastic, the man who is bound to win.

✻ ✻ ✻

How true it is, as some one says, that true salesmanship consists in *selling goods that*

SALES POINTERS 259

don't come back to people who do. This is the whole story. Selling goods that give perfect satisfaction in such a pleasing, attractive way that the customer comes back; leaving a pleasant taste in the customer's mouth, pleasant pictures in his memory of the way you treated him, so that he will put himself out to look you up the next time, this is the salesmanship which every one can cultivate. One doesn't need to be a born salesman to do this. Every one can treat a customer kindly, pleasantly, with a cheerful, helpful manner, in an accommodating spirit. The best part of salesmanship can be acquired.

❧ ❧ ❧

Winning back a customer who had quit buying of your house because you have offended him, or because he thinks the house did not treat him right, is a tough proposition. It is not every salesman who can successfully tackle such a job as this. It takes great tact and a lot of diplomacy, and yet a diplomacy that does not show itself. The art of arts is to conceal art. A great diplomat leaves no visible trace of his diplomacy. It will pay to acquire the art of the diplomats. It will pay better to avoid offending customers.

SELLING THINGS

"We broke all output records to-day." This was the message Andrew Carnegie's superintendent sent him one day. *"Why not do it every day?"* wired back the ironmaster. Why not beat your sales record every day? You don't know what you can do until you try.

✢ ✢ ✢

"The salesman that tries to sell, without using his upper story, has a lot of good loft space unoccupied."

✢ ✢ ✢

To be a conqueror in appearance, in one's bearing, is the first step toward success.

Walk, talk and act as though you were a somebody. Let victory speak from your face and express itself in your manner.

✢ ✢ ✢

Every dishonest trick, every deception, every unfair transaction, is a boomerang which comes back to hit the thrower.

✢ ✢ ✢

You should make your prospect feel that you are a real friend, that you are something more than an ordinary seller of merchandise, that you are trying to be of real service to him,

Sales Pointers

261

and that you would not take the slightest advantage of him in any way. A man's friendship should be worth a great deal to you, whether you get the particular order you are after or not.

✣ ✣ ✣

The "selling sense" is to the salesman what the "nose for news" is to the journalist. No knowledge, however profound, of mere technical salesmanship will make a salesman of you if you lack selling sense, into which many factors enter,—such as tact, spirit of kindliness, good fellowship, good judgment, levelheadedness, horse sense, initiative, courage.

✣ ✣ ✣

Like the good things you eat, a superb quality leaves a good taste in the mouth. The article that is a little better than others of the same kind, the article that is best, even though the price is higher, "carries in its first sale the possibilities of many sales, because it makes a satisfied customer, and only a satisfied customer will come again."

✣ ✣ ✣

Staying power is the final test of ability. The real caliber of a man is measured by the

262 SELLING THINGS

amount of opposition that it would take to down him. The world measures a man largely by his breaking down point. Where does he give up? How much punishment can he stand? How long can he take his medicine without running up the white flag? How much resisting power is there in him? What does the man do after he has been knocked down? This is the test.

Where is *your* giving up point, *your* breaking point, *your* turning back point? This will determine everything in your career.

✢ ✢ ✢

If you represent a large house, make a careful study of the top-notchers and cracker-jack salesmen in your firm. Study their history, their methods; get at the secret of their great success and their big salaries. The study of men above you will whet your ambition, will sharpen your perceptions and will make you more ambitious, more determined to win out, and this will enable you to make an impression of progressiveness upon your firm. They will see that you are growing, that you are reaching out, that you have no idea of getting into a rut or becoming petrified in your methods.

✢ ✢ ✢

Sales Pointers 263

Thomas Brackett Reed, the famous Speaker of the House of Representatives for many years, used to say that one-half of the battle in Congress is to get the speaker's eye. Get your prospect's eye first of all, and then you will not only get his attention, but you will interest and hold him. No other feature has such power to command and hold as the eye.

It is said that the moment a wild beast tamer shows the slightest signs of fear when he enters a cage of wild animals his game is up. They will leap upon him and kill him. The animals watch the trainer's eye and they can very quickly tell when he has lost his courage or shows the slightest sign of fear.

✣ ✣ ✣

Remember that suggestion is the soul of salesmanship. The first thing you should do when you go into a prospect's office is to suggest harmony, good will. Antidote all possible antagonism, kill prejudice. A pleasing personality is all suggestion. Suggestion is the soul of advertising, and to sell you must advertise. A salesman must be his own advertisement.

✣ ✣ ✣

264 SELLING THINGS

"JUST KEEP ON, KEEPIN' ON."

If the day looks kinder gloomy
  And your chances kinder slim;
If the situation's puzzlin',
  And the prospects awful grim;
And the prospects keep pressin'
  Till all hope is nearly gone,
Just bristle up and grit your teeth,
  And keep on, keepin' on.

Fumin' never wins a fight,
  And frettin' never pays;
There ain't no use in broodin'
  In these pessimistic ways.
Smile just kinder cheerfully,
  When hope is nearly gone,
'And bristle up and grit your teeth,
  And keep on, keepin' on.

There ain't no use of growlin',
  And grumblin' all the time,
When music's ringing everywhere,
  And everything's a rhyme.
Just keep on smiling cheerfully,
  If hope is nearly gone,
And bristle up and grit your teeth,
  And keep on, keepin' on.—SELECTED.

✻ ✻ ✻

All salesmen may take to themselves the following advice on promises, printed by Gimbel Brothers, for the benefit of all employees of their New York store.—

SALES POINTERS 265

"MAKE no promises which you cannot fulfill."

"Every individual connected with this establishment is hereby instructed not to make promises which cannot be absolutely satisfied. *You must fulfill at all costs those promises you do make, in behalf of this business.*"

✣ ✣ ✣

"He who is content to rest upon his laurels, will soon have laurels resting upon him."

✣ ✣ ✣

"A sour clerk will turn the sweetest customer."

✣ ✣ ✣

"A real salesman is one part talk and nine parts judgment; and he uses the nine parts of judgment to tell when to use the one part of talk."

✣ ✣ ✣

Whenever you say "Good morning," "Good afternoon," or "Good evening," let your words be not only cheerful, but sincere. The only was to be genuinely sincere is through cultivating a genuinely friendly disposition. It is hard to fake sincerity. Many salesmen think they can, but they only fool themselves.

266   SELLING THINGS

Learn to love mankind as a whole, and you will then be able to be genuinely sincere with each unit in humanity.

❊ ❊ ❊

"Never explain the nature of your business on the door-step—that is, before you are advantageously placed in the presence of your prospect.—Expect to get in, and you will." These are the words of an expert in salesmanship. Every expert realizes how full of truth they are.

❊ ❊ ❊

A salesman must be self-possessed, which means that he should have no fears. Keep before your mind constantly these facts: You are all right; your goods are all right, and your house is all right; therefore you have no cause for fear; you have every reason to be serene.

❊ ❊ ❊

Keep your samples out of sight as much as possible, even for your regular trade. Many salesmen leave their samples at the hotel, and call first on prospective customers, making an appointment for a certain hour. This is very effective, where possible. The display of goods is, unquestionably, very helpful in sell-

SALES POINTERS 267

ing, but it is a decided advantage to have part of the stock out of sight. The element of curiosity comes in, and, as we have explained, this helps to get the right kind of attention.

⁂

Carrying a cigar or a cigarette, even though freshly lighted, usually detracts from a man's appearance. A tooth-pick in evidence is always very bad taste, and often it has been fatal to sales. Newspapers stuck into pockets, or carried in one's hand, suggest that a man is not all there, that he is thinking more of the topics of the day than of his business. They are evidence of lack of concentration, and more often than the salesman may think he handicaps himself by having these in sight.

⁂

Jake Daubert, the well known authority in baseball, has concluded an article on his specialty with these strong words of advice: *"Always know ahead of time what you must do with the ball after you get it."* To a salesman I would say—think out all possible difficulties that may arise during the progress of a prospective sale. Be prepared for every

268 SELLING THINGS

emergency. Cultivate patience, calmness, and celerity, for they give a powerful advantage to their possessor.

❉ ❉ ❉

Seizing the psychological moment is of great importance. Admiral Dewey seized it very effectively when he gave the command, "You may fire when you are ready, Gridley." A salesman can win by *"firing"* at the right moment. He can, likewise, and should, stop *"firing"* and close the deal at the right moment. It is all psychological—a matter of mind meeting mind.

❉ ❉ ❉

Avoid as much as possible technical terms, unless you are talking to customers who, you are sure, understand them. For instance, a Life Insurance salesman makes a great mistake ordinarily, to talk about "legal reserve," "accrued dividends," "extended insurance," "paid-up values," "accelerative endowments," "expense ratios," "percentages of increase," etc. As a matter of fact, it is quite probable that a large number of those to whom he talks will not understand even the words "liabilities" and "assets."

❉ ❉ ❉

SALES POINTERS

Many a salesman has been ruined or seriously injured by carrying a side line. All of the great things of the world have been accomplished by concentration upon a specialty.

✢ ✢ ✢

A good tip to both young and old salesmen is, to study the business producers both in your firm and out of your firm. Examine their methods; learn to do what they have found effective; benefit by their strong points; but beware of their weaknesses, for even the most successful salesman will be found to have certain weak points, at times. You can quickly and conclusively recognize these. Guard against them. While you can learn much from older and more experienced salesmen, never be a slavish copy of any one. Whatever you do be yourself.

✢ ✢ ✢

Every time a man who is trying to hold an audience turns his eye from it he cuts the magnetic current which is flowing between them and if he does this often the people will get uneasy; they will begin to move in their seats and he will lose his power over them.— His magnetic connection with those he ad-

270 SELLING THINGS

dresses is made through the eye. The trained speaker knows this, and unlike the amateur who, from sheer nervousness, often looks down to the floor, or refers to his notes when it is not absolutely necessary to do so, he avoids everything that would tend to break the magnetic current between himself and his audience.

Just here is a hint for the salesman. It is imperative that you should keep this current between yourself and your prospect flowing freely. An attractive personality added to the constant flow of magnetism through your eye will rivet his attention and add immensely to your selling power.

✻ ✻ ✻

THE SALESMAN'S IDEAL

I want my Selling Talk to be a Service Talk —one that will be worth others' time whether they buy my goods or not.

I want it to tell only the truth, and that as fully as may be.

To be a perfectly human statement easily understood by others.

To show simply and plainly how both I and my goods can serve.

SALES POINTERS

To contain Wit only as that conforms to Wisdom.

To be presented in full view of the fact that every man's time is his property—only to be secured by honest methods.

To result from personal self-persuasion, as I would wish to persuade others.

To prove of such real value to patrons that my goods shall be always to the fore rather than myself.

To so demonstrate the Merits of my goods and service, that others will crave them when in need of either.

This is my ideal.—SELECTED.

✤ ✤ ✤

WHY THIS SALESMAN DID NOT SUCCEED

He was too anxious.

He could not read human nature.

He did not know how to approach his prospect.

There was not a real man back of the solicitor.

He scattered too much; could not concentrate his talk.

He knew enough, but could not tell it in an interesting way.

272 SELLING THINGS

He tired the prospect out before he got down to business, and could not see when he was boring him.

He went to his prospective customer in the spirit of "I will try" instead of "I will."

He could not take a rebuff good-naturedly.

He ran down his competitor and disgusted his prospect.

He did not believe he could get an order when he went for it.

He tried to make circulars and letters do the work of a personal canvass.

He unloaded cheap lines and off-style goods on one customer and then bragged about it to the next.

He did not thoroughly believe in the thing he was trying to sell, and of course could not convince others.

He was too easily discouraged; if he did not secure orders from the first man he solicited, he lost heart and gave up.

He did not concentrate on one line. He carried side lines. He thought if he could not sell one thing, he could another.

He did not have enough reserve argument to overcome objections. He lacked resourcefulness.

SALES POINTERS 273

He had to spend most of his time trying to overcome a bad first impression.

He gave the impression that he was a beggar instead of the representative of a reliable house.

He did not look out for the man at the other end of the bargain.

He overcanvassed. He said so many good things about the article he was selling that the prospect did not believe they were true.

He was polite only while he thought he was going to get an order, but when turned down, got mad and said disagreeable, cutting things.

He lacked tact or the power of adaptability; he always used the same line of argument, no matter what the man's position, degree of intelligence, temperament or mood might be.

He did not have a proper appreciation of the dignity of his work. He thought people would look upon him as a peddler.

He did not like the business; his heart was not in it; and he intended working at it only until he could get a better job.

He never liked to mix with people, and therefore was not popular.

He did not organize himself, could not work to a plan, had no program.

274 SELLING THINGS

He introduced politics and his fads in business.

He didn't realize that every sale is an advertisement for or against the house.

He was always gloomy and despondent. He carried his samples in a hearse.

He did not believe it paid to be accommodating.

✣ ✣ ✣

WHY THIS SALESMAN SUCCEEDED

He thoroughly believed in the things he was trying to sell.

He was tactful and knew how to approach people.

He did not waste a customer's time but was quick to the point.

He concentrated on what he was selling.

He was reliable and gave one the impression that he stood for good merchandise.

He approached a customer with the conviction that he would win his order and he usually did.

He worked hard.

SALES POINTERS

He was always looking out for the man at the other end of the bargain.

He stopped when he had convinced his prospect and did not raise doubts by boring him.

THE END

PRESS REVIEWS OF
The Young Man Entering Business

"A readable volume

on a substantial topic, which discusses actual questions. The counsel of an experienced person." *Pittsburgh Post.*

Abounds in Specific Advice

" We can easily conceive that a young man who gets this book into his hands may, in after life, date his success from reading it. It is sound, wholesome, stimulating. The treatment is concrete. It abounds in specific advice and telling illustration." *Southern Observer.*

Stimulates and Encourages

" Packed as it is with sensible, practical counsels, this volume can be cordially recommended to stimulate and encourage young men starting out in business life." *Brooklyn Times.*

A Necessity to Earnest Young Men

"There is such a thing as the science of success. Dr. Marden has made a study of it. He writes in simple, attractive style. He deals with facts. The book should be in the hands of every earnest young man." *Christian Advocate.*

Entertaining as Well as Helpful

" So interwoven with personal incident and illustration that it is an entertaining as well as a helpful book." *Christian Observer.*

Opinions and Reviews of Dr. Marden's
The Secret of Achievement

Exasperating

"'The Secret of Achievement' is one of those exasperating books which you feel you ought to present to your young friends, yet find yourself unwilling to part with." WILLIAM B. WARREN, *Former President Boston University.*

Art of Putting Things

"I have studied Dr. Marden's books with deep interest. He has the art of putting things; of planting in the mind convictions that will live. I know of no works that contain equal inspiration for life."
HEZEKIAH BUTTERWORTH.

A Great Service

"I thoroughly feel that you are rendering a great service to young men and women in America and throughout the world."
REV. R. S. MCARTHUR, D.D., *New York City.*

The Difference

"'Pushing to the Front' is a great book and 'Rising in the World' is a magnificent book, but 'The Secret of Achievement' is a superb book."

Success against Odds

"This volume contains a series of stimulating anecdotes and advice showing how energy, force of well-directed will, application, lofty purpose, and noble ideals serve to win success even against the greatest odds. Many a young man will draw inspiration from it which will aid him in making his life work a success."
School Journal.

The Victorious Attitude

By ORISON SWETT MARDEN

A Soul Doctor

"This book should be read by all discouraged people. It is a tonic—and a moral bracer of the first order. Most of us need to have our self-confidence stimulated, and Dr. Marden stimulates it. He is a soul doctor."
Richmond Times Dispatch.

Buoyant and Breezy

"Full of fresh ideas, couched in straightforward language. Buoyant, breezy and highly stimulating." *San Francisco Bulletin.*

A Wallet of Truth

"There is a crammed wallet of truth in your book. May it go forth to inspire men with the fine courage of life." *Edwin Markham.*

Excellent Advice

"The homely truths and excellent bits of advice contained in Dr. Marden's book will make instructive reading. It is written in forcible and easily understandable style." *Buffalo Commercial.*

Cannot Fail to Help

"Clear, direct and vigorous in expression, and so uplifting and wholesome in subject matter, that it cannot fail to be of help to many people who are in need of just such advice."
Des Moines Register.

Nothing More Valuable

"One of the very best books that you ever produced. The book is like a medicine to me. I commended it to our students, put it in our library, and it has been in great demand. I know of nothing finer or more valuable for young people who are struggling for an education."
Rev. O. S. Kriebel, D.D.

OPINIONS OF THE
Progressive Business Man

Sound, Practical Suggestions

"Contains a lot of sound, practical suggestions worth considering by those responsible for the conduct of business enterprises."
New York Times.

Good Business Advice

"One of the best books of business advice ever published." *Albany Argus.*

Worthy of High Commendation

"A book that contains such valuable information—and there is no doubt about this being the quality of its contents—ought to be widely read and highly prized. It is worthy of high commendation." *Religious Telescope.*

An Inspiration and a Guide

"A work that should be in the hands of every business man who desires to promote the welfare of his business. It will prove both an inspiration and a guide."
Christian Work and Evangelist.

Valuable Information

"The information in this book is so valuable that it ought to have the widest possible reading. We unhesitatingly commend it to every business man." *Trojan Messenger.*

Sane and Helpful

"Like all the Marden books, it contains a sane and helpful philosophy of right conduct."
Des Moines Capital.

Opinions of

The Miracle of Right Thought

Dr. Sheldon Leavitt says:

" I wish to state that I am unusually well pleased with Dr. Marden's 'Miracle of Right Thought.' It is the best work of the author."

Ralph Waldo Trine says:

" This is one of those inspiring, reasonable and valuable books that are bringing new life and new power to so many thousands all over our country and all over the world to-day."

"You have formulated a philosophy

which must sooner or later be universally accepted. Your book shows how the right mental attitude helps one in the realization of every laudable ambition, and the value of cultivating a bright, self-reliant habit of thought. I congratulate you on it."

G. H. Sandison, *Editor, The Christian Herald.*

"It is marked by sanctified common sense;

it is in line with the advance thought of to-day, and yet it is so simple in statement that unlettered men and untrained youtns can master its best thoughts and translate them into their daily lives."

Rev. R. S. MacArthur, D.D., *New York City.*

Rev. F. E. Clark, President United Society of Christian Endeavor, says:

"I regard 'The Miracle of Right Thought' as one of Dr. Marden's very best books, and that is saying a great deal. He has struck the modern note of the power of mind over bodily conditions in a fresh and most interesting way, while he has not fallen into the mistake of some New Thought writers of eliminating the personal God from the universe. No one can read this book sympathetically, I believe, without being happier and better."

Letters to Dr. Marden concerning

Getting On

Effective and Inspiring

"I think the chapters in this book are the most effective and inspiring I have read. They make one want to be something better. Had I read them ten or fifteen years ago I should have been a different person now."
H. J. CROPLEY, *Victoria, Australia.*

"I have gained great good

from reading the chapter 'Emergencies the Test of Ability.' You have placed my ideas of life and raised my goals far above what they once were."
RUPERT C. BOWDEN, *Magazine, Arkansas.*

Of Value to Employees

"I became so impressed with the directness of your article 'The Precedent Breaker' that I shall ask each one of our employees to read it, notifying them of its appearance through our weekly bulletin."
SAMUEL BRILL, *Head of firm of Brill Bros.*

Chapter reprinted by Bell Telephone Co.

"I take pleasure in sending you two copies of *The Telephone News,* in which appears your splendid article 'The Precedent Breaker.' We are grateful for your kind permission to send this through the *News* to six thousand Bell Telephone employees."
GEORGE G. STEEL, *Advertising Manager Bell Telephone Co. of Pennsylvania.*

An Inspiration in Time of Need

"I wish to thank you for the chapter on 'Clear Grit did It.' It has been an inspiration to me in a time when I needed it most."
C. W. HALE, *Indianapolis, Ind.*

Letters to Dr. Marden concerning

Every Man a King

Success vs. Failure

"One of the most inspiring books I have ever read. I should like to purchase a thousand and distribute them, as I believe the reading of this book would make the difference between success and failure in many lives." CHAS. E. SCHMICK, *House of Representatives, Mass.*

Worth One Hundred Dollars

"I would not take one hundred dollars for your book, 'Every Man a King,' if no other were available." WILLARD MERRIAM, *New York City.*

Unfailing Optimism

"The unfailing note of optimism which rings through all your works is distinctly sounded here." W. E. HUNTINGTON, *Pres., Boston University.*

The Keynote of Life

"'Every Man a King' strikes the keynote of life. Any one of its chapters is well worth the cost of the book." E. J. TEAGARDEN, *Danbury, Conn.*

Simply Priceless

"I have just read it with tremendous interest, and I frankly say that I regard it as simply priceless. Its value to me is immeasurable, and I should be glad if I could put it in the hands of every intelligent young man and woman in this country." CHAS. STOKES WAYNE, *Chappaqua, N. Y.*

Renewed Ambition

"I have read and re-read it with pleasure and renewed ambition. I shall ever keep it near at hand as a frequent reminder and an invaluable text-book." H. H. WILLIAMS, *Brockton, Mass.*

Letters to Dr. Marden concerning

Ibe Can Wbo Tbinks Ibe Can

Will Do Amazing Good

"I believe ' He Can Who Thinks He Can,' comprising some of your editorials, which appear akin to divine inspiration in words of cheer, hope, courage and success, will do amazing good."
JAMES PETER, *Independence, Kas.*

Greatest Things Ever Written

"Your editorials on the subjects of self-confidence and self-help are the greatest things ever written along that line." H. L. DUNLAP, *Waynesburg, Pa.*

Gripping Power

"Presents the truth in a remarkably clear and forcible manner, with a gripping power back of the writing. It is beautiful and inspiring."
C. W. SMELSER, *Coopertown, Okla.*

Beginning of My Success

"Your editorials have helped me more than any other reading. The beginning of my success was when I commenced to practise your teachings."
BRUCE HARTMAN, *Honolulu, T. H.*

Wishes to Reprint It

"I have been very much impressed by the chapter on 'New Thought, New Life.' I would like to send a copy of it to two thousand of my customers, giving due credit of course." JOHN D. MORRIS, *Philadelphia, Pa.*

Full of Light and Joy

"I have studied the subject of New Thought for ten years, but have never seen anything so comprehensive, so full of light and joy, as your treatment of it. When I think of the good it will do, and the thousands it will reach, my heart rejoices."
LOUISE MARKSCHEFFEL, *Toledo, O.*

Press Reviews of Dr. Marden's
Be Good to Yourself

"The author is a wonder,—

one of the very best preachers. through the pen, of our time." *Zion's Herald.*

"Just such a discussion of personality

as we all need. The titles of the chapters are appetizing and the advice and lessons taught are good. It will help many a reader to understand himself better." *The Advance.*

"The kind counsel of a new book

by Orison Swett Marden, who says there are many people who are good to others but not to themselves. This is a fine volume from every point of view." *The Religious Telescope.*

"Of a thoroughly inspirational character,

these essays are calculated to awaken and sustain the right sort of ambition and evolve a manly type of character. They are surcharged with faith, optimism, and common sense." *The Boston Herald.*

"Dr. Marden's friends,

who are to be found in all quarters of the globe, wait eagerly for such advice as this, on how to be happy, hearty, and healthy." *Seattle Post-Intelligencer.*

LETTERS ABOUT

𝔓eace, 𝔓ower and 𝔓lenty

"I cannot thank you enough for 'Peace, Power and Plenty.' Your former book, 'Every man a King,' has been my 'bedside book' for many months now,—the new one is even more of a comfort."—BLANCHE BATES.

"I have read with great pleasure, interest and profit your admirable 'Peace, Power and Plenty.' To have written such a book is a service to the race."—CHARLES EDWARD RUSSELL.

Andrew Carnegie says

"I thank you for 'Why Grow Old?' (a chapter in 'Peace, Power and Plenty')."

John Burroughs says

"I am reading a chapter or two in 'Peace, Power and Plenty' each evening. You preach a sound, vigorous, wholesome doctrine."

"The most valuable chapter for me"

says Thomas Wentworth Higginson, "is that on 'Why Grow Old?' I wish to learn just that. I am now 85, and have never felt old yet, but I shall keep your chapter at hand in case that should ever happen to me."

Conan Doyle says

"I find it very stimulating and interesting."

"The chapter on 'Health Through Right Thinking' alone is worth five hundred dollars." —SAMUEL BRILL, Head of the firm of Brill Brothers, New York.

Letters to Dr. Marden concerning

𝔓ushing to the 𝔉ront

What President McKinley Said

"It cannot but be an inspiration to every boy or girl who reads it, and who is possessed of an honorable and high ambition. Nothing that I have seen of late is more worthy to be placed in the hands of the American youth." WILLIAM MCKINLEY.

An English View

"I have read 'Pushing to the Front' with much interest. It would be a great stimulus to any young man entering life." SIR JOHN LUBBOCK.

A Powerful Factor

"This book has been a powerful factor in making a great change in my life. I feel that I have been born into a new world." ROBERT S. LIVINGSTON, *Deweyville, Tex.*

The Helpfulest Book

"'Pushing to the Front' is more of a marvel to me every day. I read it almost daily. It is the helpfulest book in the English language." MYRON T. PRITCHARD, *Boston, Mass.*

A Practical Gift

"It has been widely read by our organization of some fifteen hundred men. I have personally made presents of more than one hundred copies." E. A. EVANS, *President Chicago Portrait Co.*

Its Weight in Gold

"If every young man could read it carefully at the beginning of his career it would be worth more to him than its weight in gold." R. T. ALLEN, *Billings, Mon.*

SUN BOOKS • SUN PUBLISHING

Sun Books
Sun Publishing
Supplement B-4

Booklist of these fine Authors:
James Allen
Christian D. Larson
Orison Swett Marden
Ralph Waldo Trine

JAMES ALLEN TITLES

ABOVE LIFE'S TURMOIL by James Allen. True Happiness, Immortal Man, Overcoming of Self, Uses of Temptation, Basis of Action, Belief that Saves, Thought and Action, Your Mental Attitude, The Supreme Justice, Use of Reason, Self-Discipline, Resolution, Contentment in Activity, Pleasant Pastures of Peace, Etc. 163p. 5X8. Paperback. ISBN 0-89540-203-3.

ALL THESE THINGS ADDED by James Allen. Entering the Kingdom, Soul's Great Need, At Rest in the Kingdom, The Heavenly Life, Divine Center, Eternal Now, "Original Simplicity", The Might of Meekness, Perfect Love, Greatness and Goodness, and Heaven in the Heart, Etc. 192p. 5X8. Paperback. ISBN 0-89540-129-0.

AS A MAN THINKETH by James Allen. Thought and Character, Effect of Thought on Circumstances, Effect of Thought on Health and the Body, Thought and Purpose, The Thought-Factor in Achievement, Visions and Ideals, Serenity. 88p. 5X8. Paperback. ISBN 0-89540-136-3.

BYWAYS OF BLESSEDNESS by James Allen. Right Beginnings, Small Tasks and Duties, Transcending Difficulties, Hidden Sacrifices, Sympathy, Forgiveness, Seeing No Evil, Abiding Joy, Silentness, Solitude, Understanding the Simple Laws of Life, Happy Endings, Etc. 202p. 5X8. Paperback. ISBN 0-89540-202-5.

THE DIVINE COMPANION by James Allen. Truth as Awakener, Truth as Protector, Of Discipline and Purification, Of Purity of Heart, The First Prophecy- Called Awakening, The Fifth Prophecy- Called Transition, The Second Exhortation- Concerning Humility, Instruction Concerning the Great Reality, Discourse Concerning The Way of Truth, Self-Restraint, Etc. 152p. 5X8. Paperback. ISBN 0-89540-329-3.

EIGHT PILLARS OF PROSPERITY by James Allen. Discussion on Energy, Economy, Integrity, Systems, Sympathy, Sincerity, Impartiality, Self-reliance, and the Temple of Prosperity. 233p. 5X8. Paperback. ISBN 0-89540-201-7.

ENTERING THE KINGDOM by James Allen. The Soul's Great Need, The Competitive Laws and the Laws of Love, The Finding of a Principle, At Rest in the Kingdom, And All Things Added. 82p. 5X8. Paperback. ISBN 0-89540-226-2.

FOUNDATION STONES TO HAPPINESS AND SUCCESS by James Allen. Right Principles, Sound Methods, True Actions, True Speech, Equal Mindedness, Good Results. 53p. 5X8. Paperback. ISBN 0-89540-327-7.

FROM PASSION TO PEACE by James Allen. Passion, Aspiration, Temptation, Transmutation, Transcendence, Beatitude, Peace. 64p. 5X8. Paperback. ISBN 0-89540-077-4.

FROM POVERTY TO POWER by James Allen. The Path to Prosperity, Way Out of Undesirable Conditions, Silent Power of Thought, Controlling and Directing One's Forces, Secret of Health, Success, and Power, The Way of Peace, Power of Meditation, Self and Truth, Spiritual Power, Realization of Selfless Love, Entering into the Infinite, Perfect Peace, Etc. 184p. 5X8. Paperback. ISBN 0-89540-061-8.

THE HEAVENLY LIFE by James Allen. The Divine Center, The Eternal Now, "Original Simplicity", Unfailing Wisdom, Might of Meekness, The Righteous Man, Perfect Love, Perfect Freedom, Greatness and Goodness, Heaven in the Heart. 84p. 5X8. Paperback. ISBN 0-89540-227-0.

THE LIFE TRIUMPHANT by James Allen. Faith and Courage, Manliness and Sincerity, Energy and Power, Self-Control and Happiness, Simplicity and Freedom, Right-Thinking and Repose, Calmness and Resource, Insight and Nobility, Man and the Master, and Knowledge and Victory. 114p. 5X8. Paperback. ISBN 0-89540-125-8.

LIGHT ON LIFE'S DIFFICULTIES by James Allen. The Light that Leads to Perfect Peace, Law of Cause and Effect in Human Life, Values- Spiritual and Material, Adherence to Principle, Management of the Mind, Self-Control, Acts and their Consequences, Way of Wisdom, Individual Liberty, Blessing and Dignity of Work, Diversity of Creeds, War and Peace, Brotherhood of Man, Life's Sorrows, Life's Change, Etc. 137p. 5X8. Paperback. ISBN 0-89540-127-3.

MAN: KING OF MIND, BODY AND CIRCUMSTANCE by James Allen. Inner World of Thoughts, Outer World of Things, Habit: Its Slavery and Its Freedom, Bodily Conditions, Poverty, Man's Spiritual Dominion, Conquest: Not Resignation. 55p. 5X8. Paperback. ISBN 0-89540-212-2.

MEN AND SYSTEMS by James Allen. Men and Systems, Work, Wages, and Well-Being, The Survival of the Fittest as Divine Law, Justice in Evil, Justice and Love, Self-Protection- Animal, Human, and Divine, Aviation and the New Consciousness, The New Courage. 149p. 5X8. Paperback. ISBN 0-89540-326-9.

THE MASTERY OF DESTINY by James Allen. Deeds, Character and Destiny, Science of Self-Control, Cause and Effect in Human Conduct, Training of the Will, Thoroughness, Mind-Building and Life-Building, Cultivation of Concentration, Practice of Meditation, Power of Purpose, Joy of Accomplishment. 120p. 5X8. Paperback. ISBN 0-89540-209-2.

MEDITATIONS, A YEAR BOOK by James Allen. "James Allen may truly be called the Prophet of Meditation. In an age of strife, hurry, religious controversy, heated arguments, ritual and ceremony, he came with his message of Meditation, calling men away from the din and strife of tongues into the peaceful paths of stillness within their own souls, where 'the Light that lighteth every man that cometh into the world' ever burns steadily and surely for all who will turn their weary eyes from the strife without to the quiet within." Contains two quotes and a brief commentary for each day of the year. 366p. 5X8. Paperback. ISBN 0-89540-192-4.

MORNING AND EVENING THOUGHTS by James Allen. Contains a separate and brief paragraph for each morning and evening of the month. 71p. 5X8. Paperback. ISBN 0-89540-137-1.

OUT FROM THE HEART by James Allen. Heart and the Life, Nature of Power of Mind, Formation of Habit, Doing and Knowing, First Steps in the Higher Life, Mental Conditions and Their Effects, Exhortation. 54p. 5X8. Paperback. ISBN 0-89540-228-9.

THE SHINING GATEWAY by James Allen. The Shining Gateway of Meditation, Temptation, Regeneration, Actions and Motives, Morality and Religion, Memory, Repetition and Habit, Words and Wisdom, Truth Made Manifest, Spiritual Humility, Spiritual Strength, Etc. 58p. 5X8. Paperback. ISBN 0-89540-328-5.

THROUGH THE GATE OF GOOD by James Allen. The Gate and the Way, Law and the Prophets, The Yoke and the Burden, The Word and the Doer, The Vine and the Branches, Salvation this Day. 66p. 5X8. Paperback. ISBN 0-89540-216-5.

THE WAY OF PEACE by James Allen. The Power of Meditation, The Two Masters: Self and Truth, Spiritual Power, Realization of Selfless Love, Entering into the Infinite, Saints, Sages and Saviors, The Law of Service, Realization of Perfect Peace. 113p. 5X8. Paperback. ISBN 0-89540-229-7.

PERSONALITY: IT'S CULTIVATION AND POWER AND HOW TO ATTAIN by Lily L. Allen. Personality, Right Belief, Self-Knowledge, Intuition, Decision and Promptness, Self-Trust, Thoroughness, Manners, Physical Culture, Mental, Moral and Spiritual Culture, Introspection, Emancipation, Self-Development, Self-Control and Mental Poise, Liberty, Transformation, Balance, Meditation and Concentration. 170p. 5X8. Paperback. ISBN 0-89540-218-1.

CHRISTIAN D. LARSON

BRAINS AND HOW TO GET THEM by Christian D. Larson. Building the Brain, Making Every Brain Cell Active, Principles in Brain Building, Practical Methods in Brain Building, Vital Secrets in Brain Building, Special Brain Development, The Inner Secret, The Finer Forces, Subjective Concentration, Principle of Concentration, Development of Business Ability, Accumulation and Increase, Individual Advancement, The Genius of Invention, The Musical Prodigy, Talent and Genius in Art, Talent and Genius in Literature, Vital Essentials in Brain Building. 233p. 5X8. Paperback. ISBN 0-89540-382-X.

YOUR FORCES AND HOW TO USE THEM by Christian D. Larson. How We Govern the Forces We Possess, The Use of Mind in Pratical Action, Training the Subconscious for Special Results, How Man Becomes What He Thinks, He Can Who Thinks He Can, How We Secure What We Persistently Desire, Concentration and the Power of Suggestion, The Development of the Will, The Building of a Great Mind, How Character Determines Constructive Action, The Creative Forces in Man, Imagination and the Master Mind, Ect. 331p. 5X8. Paperback. ISBN 0-89540-380-3.

ORISON SWETT MARDEN

AMBITION AND SUCCESS by Orison Swett Marden. What is Ambition?, The Satisfied Man, The Influence of Environment, Unworthy Ambitions, Ambition Knows No Age Limit, Make Your Life Count, Visualize Yourself in a Better Position, Thwarted Ambition, Why Don't You Begin?. 75p. 5X8. Paperback. ISBN 0-89540-369-2.

BE GOOD TO YOURSELF by Orison Swett Marden. Be Good to Yourself, Where Does Your Energy Go?, The Strain to Keep Up Appearances, Nature as a Joy Builder, The Right to be Disagreeable, The Good Will Habit, Keeping a Level Head, Getting the Best Out of Employees, Don't Let Your Past Spoil Your Future, The Passion for Achievement, Neglect Your Business But Not Your Boy, The Home as a School of Good Manners, Self Improvement as Investment, Etc. 322p. 5X8. Paperback. ISBN 0-89540-364-1.

CHARACTER - The Grandest Thing in the World by Orison Swett Marden. A Grand Character, The Light Bearers, The Great-Hearted, Intrepidity of Spirit, "A Fragment of the Rock of Ages," Etc. 55p. 5X8. Paperback. ISBN 0-89540-297-1.

CHEERFULNESS AS A LIFE POWER by Orison Swett Marden. What Vanderbilt Paid for Twelve Laughs, The Cure for Americanitis, Oiling Your Business Machinery, Taking Your Fun Every Day as You Do Your Work, Finding What You Do Not Seek, "Looking Pleasant"- A Thing to be Worked From the Inside, The Sunshine Man. 79p. 5X8. Paperback. ISBN 0-89540-363-3.

EVERY MAN A KING or Might in Mind Mastery by Orison Swett Marden. Steering Thought Prevents Life Wrecks, How Mind Rules the Body, Thought Causes Health and Disease, Overcoming Fear, Mastering our Moods, The Power of Cheerful Thinking, Affirmation Creates Power, How Thinking Brings Success, Building Character, The Power of Imagination, How to Control Thought, Etc. 240p. 5X8. Paperback. ISBN 0-89540-334-X.

THE EXCEPTIONAL EMPLOYEE by Orison Swett Marden. The Exceptional Employee, Self-Discovery, Conquering an Uncongenial Environment, The Power of Enthusiasm, Self-Confidence Gets the Job, Why A Good Appearance Wins, Getting the Position That Calls Out Your Best, Health as Business Capital, Putting Your Best into Everything, In Cheating Your Employer You Cheat Yourself, Keeping Your Working Standards Up, Gray Hairs Seeking a Job, All Work and No Play a Bad Policy, Make Your Work Your Masterpiece, Etc. 202p. 5X8. Paperback. ISBN 0-89540-352 8.

GETTING ON by Orison Swett Marden. Who Holds You Down?, A Cheery Disposition, How to Be Popular, Physical Vigor And Achievement, Begin Right- Right Away, Emergencies- the Test of Ability, Go Into Business for Yourself, The Stimulus of Rebuffs, Gentleness Versus Bluster, The Miracle of Polite Persistency, Over-Sensitivness as a Barrier, The Tragedy of Carelessness, The Love of Excellence, A Vacation as an Investment, On Commercializing One's Ability, Mere Money-Making is Not Success, Etc. 325p. 5X8. Paperback. ISBN 0-89540-370-6.

GOOD MANNERS- A PASSPORT TO SUCCESS by Orison Swett Marden. The Home Training, Self-Respect, Self-Control, Tact, The Relation of Courtesy to a Business Career, Manners in Public Life, The Law of Kindness. 64p. 5X8. Paperback. ISBN 0-89540-366-8.

HE CAN WHO THINKS HE CAN by Orison Swett Marden. He Can Who Thinks He Can, Getting Aroused, Education by Absorption, Freedom at Any Cost, What the World Owes to Dreamers, The Spirit in Which You Work, Responsibility Develops Power, Stand for Something, Happy, If Not, Why? Originality, Sizing Up People, Getting Away From Poverty, Etc. 245p. 5X8. Paperback. ISBN 0-89540-346-3.

THE HOUR OF OPPORTUNITY by Orison Swett Marden. The Hour of Opportunity: Are You Ready For It? Self-Made or Never Made, Do Not Wait For Opportunity, Self-Training, Do You Know a Good Thing When You See It?, Every-Day Opportunities, The Executive Quality, What Is My Right Place, "I Never Asked Anything About It," The Power of Adaption, Focus Your Energies, Become a Specialist, The Inspiration of a Great Purpose, Etc. 72p. 5X8. Paperback. ISBN 0-89540-336-6.

HOW THEY SUCCEEDED by Orison Swett Marden. Marshall Field, Alexander G. Bell, Helen Gould, Philip D. Armour, Mary E. Proctor, John Wanamaker, Darius Ogden Mills, Lillian Nordica, John D. Rockefeller, Julia Ward Howe, Thomas A. Edison, Lew Wallace, Andrew Carnegie, John Burroughs, James Whitcomb Riley, Etc. 365p. 5X8. Paperback. ISBN 0-89540-345-5.

HOW TO GET WHAT YOU WANT by Orison Swett Marden. How to Get What You Want, Discouragement a Disease- How to Cure It, The Force that Moves Mountains, Faith and Drugs, How to Find Oneself, How to Attract Prosperity, Heart-to-Heart Talks With Yourself, Etc. 331p. 5X8. Paperback. ISBN 0-89540-335-8.

HOW TO SUCCEED or Stepping Stones to Fame and Fortune by Orison Swett Marden. Seize Your Opportunity, How Did He Begin?, What Shall I Do?, Foundation Stones, The Conquest of Obstacles, To Be Great- Concentrate, Thoroughness, Courage and Will Power, Guard Your Weak Point, Live Upward, Moral Sunshine, Hold Up Your Head, Books and Success, Etc. 332p. 5X8. Paperback. ISBN 0-89540-371-4.

AN IRON WILL by Orison Swett Marden. Training the Will, Mental Discipline, Conscious Power, Do You Believe in Yourself? Will Power in its Relation to Health and Disease, The Romance of Achievement Under Difficulties, Concentrated Energy, Staying Power, Persistent Purpose, Success Against Odds, Etc. 49p. 5X8. Paperback. ISBN 0-89540-283-1.

LITTLE VISITS WITH GREAT AMERICANS or Success Ideals and How to Attain Them, Vol. I. by Orison Swett Marden. Thomas Alva Edison, Andrew Carnegie, Marshall Field, John Wanamaker, Darius Ogden Mills, Cornelius Vanderbilt, Samuel Gompers, Theodore Roosevelt, Nelson A. Miles, Jacob Gould Shurman, James Witcomb Riley, Ella Wheeler Wilcox, Lew Wallace, Mrs. Burton Harrison, Edwin Austin Abbey, Alice Barber Stevens, Frederic Remington, Charles Dana Gibson. Etc. 352p. 5X8. Paperback. ISBN 0-89540-372-2.

LITTLE VISITS WITH GREAT AMERICANS or Success Ideals and How to Attain Them, Vol. II. by Orison Swett Marden. Frederick Burr Opper, Marshall P. Wilder, Richard Mansfield, John Philip Sousa, Helen Keller, John Burroughs, Helen Miller Gould, Nathan Strauss, Robert Collyer, Lillian Nordica, Etc. Canadians: Robert Laird Borden, S.N. Parent, Andrew G. Blair, Sir William C. VanHorne, Etc. 389p. 5X8. Paperback. ISBN 0-89540-373-0.

LITTLE VISITS WITH GREAT AMERICANS or Success Ideals and How to Attain Them, TWO VOLUME SET by Orison Swett Marden. 741p. 5X8. Paperback. ISBN 0-89540-374-9.

MAKING LIFE A MASTERPIECE by Orison Swett Marden. Making Life a Masterpiece, Practical Dreamers, Where Your Opportunity Is, The Triumph of Common Virtues, Masterfulness and Physical Vigor, Curing the Curse of Indecision, Unlocking Your Possibilities, The Will to Succeed, The Kingship of Self Control, Finding Your Place, The Secret of Happiness, Etc. 329p. 5X8. Paperback. ISBN 0-89540-365-X.

THE MIRACLE OF RIGHT THOUGHT by Orison Swett Marden. Working for One Thing and Expecting Something Else, Expect Great Things of Yourself, Self-Encouragement by Self-Suggestion, Change the Thought- Change the Man, The Paralysis of Fear, Getting in Tune, A New Way of Bringing Up Children, Training for Longevity, As A Man Thinketh, Etc. 339p. 5X8. Paperback. ISBN 0-89540-311-0.

THE OPTIMISTIC LIFE by Orison Swett Marden. The Power of Amiability, The Inner Life as Related to Outward Beauty, The Value of Friends, The Cost of an Explosive Temper, Learn to Expect a Great Deal of Life, Mental Power, If You Can Talk Well, Brevity and Directness, What Distinguishes Work From Drudgery, Keeping Fit for Work, Mastering Moods, Business Integrity, Wresting Triumph from Defeat, Freshness in Work, Don't Take Your Business Troubles Home, Let It Go, Etc. 316p. 5X8. Paperback. ISBN: 0-89540-351-X.

PEACE, POWER, AND PLENTY by Orison Swett Marden. The Power of the Mind to Compel the Body, Poverty a Mental Disease, The Law of Opulence, Character-Building and Health-Building During Sleep, Health Through Right Thinking, Imagination and

Health, How Suggestion Influences Health, Why Grow Old?, The Miracle of Self-Confidence, Self-Control vs the Explosive Passions, Good Cheer- God's Medicine, Etc. 323p. 5X8. Paperback. ISBN 0-89540-343-9.

THE POWER OF PERSONALITY by Orison Swett Marden. What a Good Appearance Will Do, The Essentials of a Good Appearance, Cleanliness and Morals, The Importance of Dress, "The Manners Make the Man," Hindering Habits, Shyness, Personal Magnetism. 86p. 5X8. Paperback. ISBN 0-89540-362-5.

PUSHING TO THE FRONT VOL I by Orison Swett Marden. Opportunities Where You Are, Possibilities in Spare Time, How Poor Boys and Girls Go to College, Your Opportunity Confronts You- What, Will You Do With It?, Choosing a Vocation, Concentrated Energy, The Triumph of Enthusiasm, Promptness, Appearance, Personality, Common Sense, Accuracy, Persistence, Success Under Difficulties, Observation and Self-Improvement, The Triumph of the Common Virtues, Etc. 432p. 5X8. Paperback. ISBN 0-89540-331-5.

PUSHING TO THE FRONT VOL II by Orison Swett Marden. The Man With an Idea, The Will and the Way, Work and Wait, The Might of Little Things, Expect Great Things of Yourself, Stand for Something, Habit: The Servant or The Master, The Power of Purity, The Power of Suggestion, The Conquest of Poverty, The Home as a School of Good Manners, Thrift, Why Some Succeed and Others Fail, Character is Power, Rich Without Money, Etc. 441p. 5X8. Paperback. ISBN 0-89540-332-3.

PUSHING TO THE FRONT, TWO VOL. SET by Orison Swett Marden. 873p. 5x8. Paperback. ISBN: 0-89540-333-1

RISING IN THE WORLD or ARCHITECTS OF FATE by Orison Swett Marden. Dare, The Will and the Way, Uses of Obstacles, Self-Help, Work and Wait, Rich Without Money, Opportunities Where You Are, The Might of Little Things, Choosing a Vocation, The Man With an Idea, The Curse of Idleness, Etc. 318p. 5X8. Paperback. ISBN 0-89540-375-7.

THE SECRET OF ACHIEVEMENT by Orison Swett Marden. Moral Sunshine, "Blessed Be Drudgery", Honesty- As Principle and As Policy, Habit: The Servant or The Master, Courage, Self-Control, & The School of Life, Decide, Tenacity of Purpose, The Art of Keeping Well, Purity is Power, Etc. 301p. 5X8. Paperback. ISBN 0-89540-337-4.

SELF-INVESTMENT by Orison Swett Marden. If You Can- Talk Well, Put Beauty into Your Life, Enjoying What Others Own, Personality as a Success Asset, How to Be a Social Success, The Miracle of Tact, "I Had a Friend," Ambition, Education by Reading, Discrimination in Reading, Reading- A Spur to Ambition, The Self-Improvement Habit- A Great Asset, The Raising of Values, Self-Improvement Through Public Speaking, What a Good Appearance Will Do, Self-Reliance, Mental Friends and Foes. 315p. 5X8. Paperback. ISBN 0-89540-376-5.

SELLING THINGS by Orison Swett Marden. The Man Who Can Sell Things, Training the Salesman, Making a Favorable Impression, The Selling Talk or "Presentation", How to Get Attention, Friend-Winner and Business-Getter, Sizing Up the Prospect, How Suggestion Helps in Selling, The Gentle Art of Persuasion, Closing the Deal, Enthusiasm, Meeting and Forestalling Objections, Finding Customers, When You are Discouraged, Know Your Goods, Character is Capital, Keeping Fit and Salesmanship, Etc. 276p. 5X8. Paperback. ISBN 0-89540-339-0.

SUCCESS, A BOOK OF IDEALS, HELPS, AND EXAMPLES FOR ALL DESIRING TO MAKE THE MOST OF LIFE by Orison Swett Marden. Enthusiasm, Education Under Difficulties, The Game of the World, Misfit Occupations, Doing Everyting to a Finish, "Help Yourself Society," "I Will," Conduct as Fine Art, Character Building, Medicine for the Mind, "This One Thing I Do," "I Had a Friend," Ideals. 347p. 5X8. Paperback. ISBN: 0-89540-360-9.

SUCCESS NUGGETS by Orison Swett Marden. Does an Education Pay?, To Take the Drudgery Out of Your Occupation, Where Happiness is Found, Why He Was Not Promoted, Why They Are Poor, Why He Found Life Disappointing, If You Would Be Very, Very Popular, What the World Wants, Don't Wait for Your Opportunity-Make It, When is Success a Failure?, He Succeeded in Business but Failed as a Man Because..., Does a Vacation Pay?, What Message Does Your Success Bring?, The Time Will Come, Etc. 76p. 5X8. Paperback. ISBN: 0-89540-354-4.

THE VICTORIOUS ATTITUDE by Orison Swett Marden. The Victorious Attitude, "According to Thy Faith," Making Dreams Come True, Making Yourself a Prosperity Magnet, The Triumph of Health Ideals, How to Make the Brain Work for Us During Sleep, Preparing the Mind For Sleep, How to Stay Young, Our Oneness With Infinite Life, Etc. 358p. 5X8. Paperback. ISBN: 0-89540-353-6.

WHY GROW OLD? by Orison Swett Marden. Marden instructs his reader to "hold to youthful, buoyant thought" and keep the imagination alive and flexible. Recognizing that we may be slaves to our attitudes, this text encourages us to make as much of ourselves as possible and in doing so watch as our lives are prolonged. 30p. 5X8. Paperback. ISBN 0-89540-340-4.

WINNING OUT by Orison Swett Marden. Good Manners and Success, Learning to Hold Your Tounge, The Emperor Who Earned

His Own Shoe-Leather, The Boy Who Did Not Know What Time It Was, The Golconda Diamonds, Heroic Youth, The Story of the Little Red Violin, Gold Dust, Seven Hundred Books and the Farm Boy, Training for the Presidency, Send Us a Man Who Can Swim, Abraham Lincoln's Advice About Schooling, Where Does the Fun Come In?. Etc. 251p. 5X8. Paperback. ISBN 0-89540-377-3.

YOU CAN, BUT WILL YOU? by Orison Swett Marden. The Magic Mirror, The New Philosophy of Life, Connecting With the Power that Creates, You Can, But Will You?, How Do You Stand With Yourself?, The New Philosophy in Business, What Are You Thinking?, Facing Life the Right Way, How to Realize Your Ambition, The Open Door, Do You Carry Victory in Your Face? Etc. 338p. 5X8. Paperback. ISBN 0-89540-342-0.

THE YOUNG MAN ENTERING BUSINESS by Orison Swett Marden. Personal Capital and Choosing a Vocation, Avoid Misfit Occupations, Fixity of Purpose, When It Is Right to Change, Personal Appearance, Manners, Sensitivness and Success, The Power of Decision, The Value of Business Training, Promotion from Exceptional Work, The Timid Man and Self-Confidence, Born to Conquer, Getting to the Point, Looking Well an Keeping Well, Salesmanship, System and Order, Shall I Go Into Business for Myself?, Tact and the Art of Winning, People's Confidence, Other Men's Brains, The Art of Advertising, Keeping Up With the Times, Friendship and Success. Etc. 307p. 5X8. Paperback. ISBN 0-89540-378-1.

RALPH WALDO TRINE

CHARACTER BUILDING THOUGHT POWER by Ralph Waldo Trine. "Have we within our power to determine at all times what types of habits shall take form in our lives? In other words, is habit-forming, character-building, a matter of mere chance, or do we have it within our control?" 51p. 5X8. Paperback. ISBN 0-89540-251-3.

EVERY LIVING CREATURE or Heart Training Through the Animal World, by Ralph Waldo Trine. "The tender and humane passion in the human heart is too precious a quality to allow it to be hardened or effaced by practices such as we often indulge in." *Ralph Waldo Trine.* 50p. 5X8. Paperback. ISBN 0-89540-309-9.

THE GREATEST THING EVER KNOWN by Ralph Waldo Trine. The Greatest Thing Ever Known, Divine Energies in Every-Day Life, The Master's Great but Lost Gift, The Philosopher's Ripest Life Thought, Sustained in Peace and Safety Forever. 57p. 5X8. Paperback. ISBN 0-89540-274-2.

THE HIGHER POWERS OF MIND AND SPIRIT by Ralph Waldo Trine. The Silent, Subtle Building Forces of Mind and Spirit, Thought as a Force in Daily Living, The Divine Rule in the Mind and Heart, The Powerful Aid of the Mind in Rebuilding Body- How Body Helps Mind, Etc. 240p. 5X8. Paperback. ISBN 0-89540-278-5.

IN THE FIRE OF THE HEART by Ralph Waldo Trine. With the People: A Revelation, The Conditions that Hold among Us, As Time Deals with Nations, As to Government, A Great People's Movement, Public Utilities for the Public Good, Labour and Its Uniting Power, Agencies Whereby We Shall Secure the People's Greatest Good, The Great Nation, The Life of the Higher Beauty and Power. 336p. 5X8. Paperback. ISBN 0-89540-310-2.

IN THE HOLLOW OF HIS HAND by Ralph Waldo Trine. The Present Demand to Know the Truth, The Thought- The Existing Conditions- and theReligions of Jesus' Time, What Jesus Realized, Jesus' Own Statement of the Essence of Religion, Was the Church Sanctioned or Established by Jesus?, Our Debt to the Prophets of Israel, The Power- The Beauty- and the Sustaining Peace. 242p. 5X8. Paperback. ISBN 0-89540-358-7.

THE MAN WHO KNEW by Ralph Waldo Trine. The Power of Love, All is Well, That Superb Teaching of "Sin", He Teaches the Great Truth, When a Brave Man Chooses Death, Bigotry in Fear Condemns and Kills, Love the Law of Life, The Creative Power of Faith and Courage, Etc. 230p. 5X8. Paperback. ISBN 0-89540-267-X.

MY PHILOSOPHY AND MY RELIGION by Ralph Waldo Trine. This Place: Amid the Silence of the Centuries, With the Oldest Living Things, My Philosophy, My Religion, The Creed of the Open Road. 130p. 5X8. Paperback. ISBN 0-89540-349-8.

THE NEW ALIGNMENT OF LIFE by Ralph Waldo Trine. Science and Modern Research, The Modern Spiritual Revival, The Vitilising Power of the Master's Message, Modern Philosophic Thought, A Thinking's Man Religion, A Healthy Mind in a Healthy Body, The Mental Law of Habit. 228p. 5X8. Paperback. ISBN 0-89540-347-1

ON THE OPEN ROAD by Ralph Waldo Trine. "To realize always clearly that thoughts are forces, that like creates like and like attracts like, and that to determine one's thinking therefore is to determine his life." 65p. 5X8. Paperback. ISBN 0-89540-252-1.

THIS MYSTICAL LIFE OF OURS A Book of Suggestive Thoughts for Each Week Through the Year by Ralph Waldo Trine. The Creative Power of Thought, The Laws of Attraction, Prosperity, and Habit-Forming, Faith and Prayer- Their Nature, Self-Mastery

Thoughts are Forces, How We Attract Success or Failure, The Secret and Power of Love, Will- The Human and The Divine, The Secret of the Highest Power, Wisdom or Interior Illumination, How Mind Builds Body, Intuition: The Voice of the Soul, To Be at Peace, Etc! 190p. 5X8. Paperback. ISBN 0-89540-279-3.

THROUGH THE SUNLIT YEAR by Ralph Waldo Trine. A book of Suggestive Thoughts for each day of the year from the writings of Ralph Waldo Trine. 250p. 5X8. Paperback. ISBN 0-89540-350-1.

WHAT ALL THE WORLD'S A-SEEKING by Ralph Waldo Trine. The Principle, The Application, The Unfoldment, The Awakening, The Incoming, Character-Building Thought Power. 224p. 5X8. Paperback. ISBN 0-89540-359-5.

THE WINNING OF THE BEST by Ralph Waldo Trine. Which Way is Life Leaning?, The Creative Power of Thought, The Best Is the Life, The Power That Makes Us What We Are, A Basis of Philosophy and Religion, How We Will Win the Best. 100p. 5X8. Paperback. ISBN 0-89540-348-X.

ELBERT HUBBARD

A MESSAGE TO GARCIA and Other Essays by Elbert Hubbard. A Message to García, The Boy from Missouri Valley, Help Yourself by Helping the House. "He was of big service to me in telling me the things I knew, but which I did not know I knew, until he told me." *Thomas A. Edison.* 48p. 5X8. Paperback. ISBN 0-89540-305-6.

Please write for our *Religions, Oriental, and Western Mysticism Book Catalog,* and our *Motivational and Success Book Catalog* from Sun Publishing Co., P.O. Box 5588-B4, Santa Fe, NM 87502-5588 USA.

Visit our web site at http://www.sunbooks.com/

for notes

for notes

for notes

for notes